D1761288

I would like to dedicate this book to my mum Roni, who forever made sacrifices and gave up her world to raise me even when she was fighting her own battles. She has always been my number one fan and supporter and her overwhelming love and selflessness continues to inspire me every day.

And to my dad Ross for always working hard, for never getting angry even when I was naughty and for always being there to say dad jokes to lighten up every situation.

Kenkō

KITCHEN

KATE BRADLEY

hardie grant books

MELBOURNE · LONDON

CONTENTS

INTRODUCTION

My first cooking lessons (apart from the ones with my mother and nana) were in home economics, in the first year of high school. To say I was cheeky in that class would be an understatement. If you had asked the teacher then if she thought I would ever achieve anything to do with cooking she would have laughed. Don't get me wrong; I enjoyed home economics, but it was school and I hadn't really discovered my passion for cooking yet. I was more passionate about what pranks I could play with other people's food!

It was probably in the second year of high school that I really started getting into cooking and began making dinners for the family. At first I tried to master the basics. I learned how to make stir-fries, soups, curries, spaghetti and so on. I wanted to know how my mum just came home, threw things in a pot and served us up something sensational. I slowly became addicted to cooking, and would constantly think of new, exciting ideas I could try and changes to what I was already making.

I would pester my nana to write down all her recipes (in a nice little notebook my mum bought me). I wanted to be able to master the favourites that my nana would serve up – everyone loved her cooking and food, and I wanted to make people happy with food the way she did. I would ask her to teach me how to make meringues, cakes, scones and savoury dishes and would carefully watch every little thing that she did. My nana is certainly something special when it comes to food. Even though she is getting older, she still manages to serve me up something ridiculously tasty each time I visit, and every meal is always followed by a beautiful new cake (or two or three) that she has 'been wanting to test out'. She always puts the recipe cutting in front of me, or shows me the page in the magazine where she found it, and then tells me the alterations she has made. My nana is a cooking genius and, in my eyes, really is unbeatable.

I slowly became more and more determined in the kitchen as years went on. I wanted to be able to cook different cuisines and master various styles. I would set myself little challenges, and attempt different meals, hoping that I could create something magical. Being able to produce a beautiful meal by myself and seeing people's faces light up when I feed them is a feeling that is better than anything to me.

I became the girl who would flip through food magazines instead of *Vogue*. I was watching Nigella, Jamie, Nigel Slater and Heston in absolute awe of what they did. I wanted to be able to cook like these people. They were amazing!

I preferred to spend my money on ingredients and beautiful food. I didn't care about spending money on clothes or if I was in or out of fashion. I didn't want to go out partying. I cared about my family, cooking and finding a way to be as good as my culinary idols.

Food started to become my outlet. I needed it. If I didn't make something in the kitchen even for one day I got moody. When I started getting into the later high school years and puberty, when hormones started kicking well and truly into action, whenever I was feeling depressed my mum would order me into the kitchen. It was something I could do to instantly release any bad vibes I had hanging around me. It really was my meditation and the kitchen was my place for letting go. I would open a Nigella or Jamie cookbook, and it didn't matter what I would cook – at the end of it I would be feeling happy again and I would have something to share with those I loved.

As time went on, I began to change my style of cooking. My family was already healthy thanks to my beautiful mum, but my cooking was becoming a little decadent. I started to become more conscious of what I was eating and how it was affecting my body, which led to me becoming concerned that when I cooked unhealthy dishes, I was not only bringing harm to myself, I was damaging the insides of my family and friends without realising. It made me feel sick. I had been contributing to the health of these people in a negative way. Considering all I ever wanted was for my family and friends to be around, alive, happy and, most importantly, healthy, I knew things had to change. I started to research different diets, lifestyles and the dos and don'ts in terms of healthy eating.

I began by switching sugar with the plant-derived sweetener stevia, wheat flour with no-grain buckwheat flour, and butter with coconut oil. Pretty soon I was glued to my computer, books and television documentaries researching as much as I could about food for optimal health for myself and those around me and what foods were the most damaging and the ones to avoid in my cooking.

For a while I thought I couldn't cook anything. Everything I used to make contained nasties, but I didn't know what to do with these new healthier ingredients I now had in my kitchen. And so the experimenting began. I started the easiest way I knew how, which was to look at all my old favourite recipes and adapt them. Sometimes it worked, sometimes it failed miserably, but I never stopped trying.

Growing my own food is another element that is so important to my cooking. Knowing exactly where your food comes from, and knowing there are no harmful chemicals and pesticides all over it is crucial. It is sad that we try to do the right thing by buying fruit and vegetables from the supermarket. Yet they are laden with so many chemicals and have travelled so far, that what we're buying is not as nutritional as it should be.

Eating whole foods is the only 'diet' that I stick by. I don't eat processed foods and I always like to know where the food I am eating comes from – and what it does to my body. Since switching to a very healthy lifestyle, my family home now has over 80 fruit trees, a huge variety of vegetables and herbs and we even make herbal teas! It is an absolute paradise.

Everyone needs to do their own research on this, and I would not tell someone what they should or shouldn't eat as I know we are all at different stages and have different needs.

This book is a compilation of some of the recipes that first got me settled into the health world. It contains many of the favourites we know, love and are used to, but in a more nutritional and nourishing form. All the recipes are also extremely simple to make – it's hard enough having to wrap your head around everything else in life and nobody wants to come home from work and make a three-course fancy meal. It's hard switching from eating certain foods and changing your lifestyle to a more healthy one, but sometimes even harder convincing the family to eat it! I knew I had to create something that people could cook easily and be able to share with their families, knowing that they will still enjoy it. We sometimes settle for cooking unhealthy foods just because we know people will eat it. However, if it's not nutritious for their body, are we truly caring for them by feeding them food we know isn't good for them?

Everything in this book is delicious, tried, tested and beautiful. There is nothing that I have ever had trouble feeding to even the fussiest of eaters. The healthy versions are all very similar in taste to their originals, if not even tastier. Almost everything is refined sugar-free, dairy-free, gluten-free, wheat-free, egg-free and vegan. I have used whole foods that are easy to buy from your local store and items you should find easy and beneficial to introduce into your diet.

In this book you will see the use of some tinned items. This is simply to save you time. I know that tinned items are not always the ideal healthy choice, so look out for tins that say BPA-free. If you are worried about using a tinned ingredient, you can always replace it with the fresh version, but results may vary from the original recipe.

Our health is all that we have, and therefore I hope you find solace in this book, that you can see that healthy food doesn't mean just a bit of lettuce on a plate and it doesn't have to be hard or over-complicated. This is about using food at its roots and yet still celebrating our favourite classic recipes.

Kate
x x

INGREDIENT GUIDE

There may be some ingredients in the recipes that you are unfamiliar with. I have included an Ingredient guide on page 242, which provides information on some of these more unusual items. If you see a * symbol after an ingredient in a recipe, check the Ingredient guide.

BREAKFAST

Breakfast is such an important meal. It fuels us, curbs our hunger and controls our kilojoule (calorie) intake for the remainder of the day. When someone tells me they aren't a breakfast person, I'm sceptical. Why wouldn't you want to start your day out right? I know that time issues come into play a lot. 'I don't have time to make breakfast,' is said way too often. All the recipes in this section are so quick and easy that there's no excuse not to get in the kitchen and begin your day the best way possible! Breakfast should be a celebration. It should be enjoyed and it should be consumed with a smile and with company when possible. A good breakfast = a good mood, and in my books, that normally leads to a great day!

BLUEBERRY AND HEMP SEED
GRANOLA 14

COCONUT YOGHURT WITH
STEWED NECTARINES 17

CHIA PUDDING 18

OVERNIGHT PORRIDGE 3 WAYS 21

CORN FRITTERS WITH AVOCADO AND
'GOAT'S' CHEESE SMASH 25

MEDITERRANEAN BAKED BEANS 26

MEXICAN SCRAMBLED TOFU 29

APPLE PANCAKES WITH MAPLE
CASHEW ICE CREAM 30

MANGO AND COCONUT BREAD
WITH POACHED STONE FRUIT 33

BANANA CHIA BREAD 34

FRENCH TOAST WAFFLES WITH
BERRY COMPOTE 37

HAZELNUT AND CACAO BROWN
RICE CRISPS 38

MORNING FRUIT GALETTE 41

POP TARTS 42

BLUEBERRY AND HEMP SEED GRANOLA

Ahhhh granola. Such an amazing breakfast on the go, or to have freshly made and sitting there ready for the week ahead. It stores well, tastes great and is packed with so many goodies to keep you going for longer without the sugar highs and lows of a store-bought granola. I haven't met a mouth yet that doesn't like this recipe!

Serves 10
Prep time: 10 minutes
Cooking time: 15–20 minutes

150 g (5½ oz/1½ cups) gluten-free rolled
  (porridge) oats or rolled buckwheat
10 g (¼ oz/¼ cup) puffed amaranth*
30 g (1 oz/¼ cup) chia seeds*
25 g (1 oz) chopped almonds
30 g (1 oz/¼ cup) sunflower seeds
30 g (1 oz/¼ cup) hemp seeds*
30 g (1 oz/¼ cup) flaked brown rice*
20 g (¾ oz/⅓ cup) flaked coconut
½ teaspoon cinnamon
125 ml (4 fl oz/½ cup) coconut oil
125 ml (4 fl oz/½ cup) coconut nectar*
  or rice malt syrup*
55 g (2 oz/⅓ cup) dried blueberries

Preheat the oven to 180°C (350°F) and line a baking tray with baking paper.

Place all the dry ingredients, except the dried blueberries, in a large mixing bowl and combine.

Place the coconut oil and coconut nectar in a separate bowl. Heat over a double boiler or in a microwave for about 30 seconds until just melted.

Pour the liquid over the dry ingredients and mix until everything is well combined.

Spread the mixture evenly across the lined baking tray and bake for 10 minutes. Stir the ingredients around on the tray, and cook for another 5–10 minutes until golden. Remove from the oven, evenly sprinkle the dried blueberries on top and then let the granola cool completely on the tray.

Store in an airtight container or jar for up to 2 weeks.

COCONUT YOGHURT WITH STEWED NECTARINES

Coconut yoghurt is now a staple in my refrigerator. You can use it to replace dairy yoghurt for breakfasts, in your cooking or however you like. It's smooth, creamy and beyond delicious. When served alongside stewed fruit, such as nectarines as I've used here, it creates the most beautiful breakfast to start your day off on the right foot!

Serves 4
Prep time: 10 minutes, plus yoghurt
    fermenting time
Cooking time: 5–10 minutes

Coconut yoghurt
750 ml (25½ fl oz/3 cups) coconut cream
2 tablespoons liquid probiotics*
45 g (1½ oz) light coconut sugar*

Stewed nectarines
4 nectarines, stoned and sliced
2 tablespoons coconut nectar*
chopped pecans to serve

For the yoghurt, in a bowl combine the coconut cream, liquid probiotics and coconut sugar. Pour into a 750 ml (25½ fl oz/3 cup) sterilised jar, close the lid and let sit in a warm, sunny spot for 12 hours. Then place in the refrigerator and leave overnight. In the morning it will be ready to eat! The yoghurt will thicken up more each day. Keep it in the refrigerator for up to 1 week.

For the stewed nectarines, place the fruit in a small saucepan over medium heat with 80 ml (2½ fl oz/⅓ cup) water and the coconut nectar. Let simmer for 5–10 minutes until the nectarines are softened.

Serve the yoghurt with the stewed fruit and chopped pecans. Enjoy immediately.

CHIA PUDDING

Serves 1
Prep time: 10 minutes,
   plus setting time

Chia pudding is extremely easy to put together the night before, so there's no excuse not to have a nourishing and energising breakfast. This is a really simple and delicious dish that you can take on the go or relax and eat at home.

Chia pudding
30 g (1 oz/¼ cup) chia seeds*
*250 ml (8½ fl oz/1 cup) coconut
   milk*
1 tablespoon rice malt syrup
   or raw honey*
½ teaspoon vanilla extract
¼ teaspoon ground cardamom
¼ teaspoon sea salt

To serve
seeds from ¼ pomegranate
1 tablespoon pistachio nuts

Combine all the chia pudding ingredients in a bowl, glass or jar. Cover and place the bowl in the refrigerator to set overnight.

In the morning, sprinkle with the pomegranate seeds and pistachio nuts and enjoy! Eat immediately or store in the refrigerator for up to 24 hours.

TOP TO BOTTOM:
COCONUT QUINOA
PORRIDGE WITH
CHERRIES AND
SEEDS, VANILLA
OAT PORRIDGE
WITH VANILLA-
STEWED PEAR,
BUCKWHEAT
BIRCHER WITH
BERRIES AND BEE
POLLEN

OVERNIGHT PORRIDGE 3 WAYS

Each recipe serves 1
Prep time: 5–10 minutes,
    plus soaking overnight
Cooking time: 10 minutes

Porridge and winter get along like a house on fire. As soon as you feel the weather cooling down and you see frost on the front lawn, you know it's time to ditch the summer smoothies and bring out the oats and honey. Ever since I was young, there has been something so comforting about porridge for me. Apart from the weird period I went through when I was in grade one, and the only thing I would eat for breakfast was chicken 2-minute noodles, porridge has always been my thing.

VANILLA OAT PORRIDGE WITH VANILLA-STEWED PEAR

Vanilla oat porridge
35 g (1¼ oz/⅓ cup) rolled gluten-free (porridge) oats or rolled buckwheat
125 ml (4 fl oz/½ cup) soy milk or almond milk
125 g (4½ oz/½ cup) Coconut yoghurt (page 17)
1 teaspoon stevia*
1 teaspoon rice malt syrup* or raw honey
¼ teaspoon vanilla powder or 1 teaspoon vanilla extract

Vanilla-stewed pear
1 honey pear or brown pear
½ teaspoon stevia*
¼ teaspoon vanilla powder or ½ teaspoon vanilla extract
1 tablespoon coconut nectar* or rice malt syrup*
60 ml (2 fl oz/¼ cup) water

For the vanilla-stewed pear, cut the pear up into nice chunky slices, then put it in a small saucepan. Add the remaining pear ingredients, stir and cook on low heat for around 10 minutes until the pear is soft. Place the pear in a container and put in the refrigerator overnight.

Place all the porridge ingredients in a bowl and mix to combine. Cover and let the mixture sit in the refrigerator overnight.

If, in the morning, the porridge mixture is a little stiff, simply add a splash of milk or yoghurt and mix in to loosen. Place your stewed pear on top of the porridge, then heat in the microwave on High (100%) for a minute if you would like it warm, or you can eat it the way it is – it tastes delicious hot or cold!

>

COCONUT QUINOA PORRIDGE WITH CHERRIES AND SEEDS

This one is the easiest of the three recipes, and is so creamy and delicious. This is the porridge I would make for the morning if I have had quinoa for dinner, as all you have to do is set a little aside and your breakfast is half done.

100 g (3½ oz/½ cup) cooked quinoa*
90 g (3 oz/⅓ cup) coconut cream
1 teaspoon rice malt syrup*
splash of soy or almond milk, if needed
2–3 cherries, pitted
1 teaspoon pepitas (pumpkin seeds)
dried mulberries or any other fruit or
    seeds of choice

Mix the cooked quinoa with the coconut cream and rice malt syrup. If a looser consistency is desired, add a splash of milk and cover and leave in the refrigerator until the morning. In the morning pull it out of the refrigerator, top with the cherries, seeds and fruit and you're done. So easy.

BUCKWHEAT BIRCHER WITH BERRIES AND BEE POLLEN

This one again is so, so simple.

40 g (1½ oz/¼ cup) buckwheat groats*
small handful of mixed nuts (walnuts
    and almonds are my favourite)
1 small green apple, grated
juice of ½ orange
1 tablespoon coconut cream or
    vegan yoghurt
1 teaspoon stevia* or rice malt syrup*
¼ teaspoon vanilla powder or
    ½ teaspoon vanilla extract
pinch of cardamom
pinch of cinnamon
pinch of nutmeg
berries to serve
bee pollen* to serve (optional)
pomegranate seeds to serve (optional)
coconut flakes to serve (optional)

Soak your buckwheat and nuts overnight in water. Then, in the morning, place all the ingredients, except the ones to serve, in a food processor and blitz until quite smooth. To serve, top with berries and bee pollen, pomegranate seeds and coconut flakes for a little crunch, if desired.

CORN FRITTERS WITH AVOCADO AND 'GOAT'S' CHEESE SMASH

I couldn't not include these corn fritters in my cookbook, not only because they are a staple in my house and my mother's absolute favourite, but because they are so simple and packed with goodness. You can even make these the night before and just heat them up in the morning, or you can cook them and eat one or two as a snack throughout a busy day.

Serves 2–3 (makes 6–9 fritters)
Prep time: 5 minutes
Cooking time: 25–30 minutes

Corn fritters
400 g (14 oz/2⅔ cups) organic corn kernels
65 g (2¼ oz/½ cup) buckwheat flour
2 flax eggs* ('no egg' replacement mix)
2 spring onions (scallions), chopped
½ teaspoon salt
½ teaspoon freshly ground black pepper
1 tablespoon chopped flat-leaf parsley
60 ml (2 fl oz/¼ cup) plant-based oil*

Avocado and 'goat's' cheese smash
½ avocado, stoned
30 g (1 oz/¼ cup) Cashew 'goat's' cheese (page 220)
juice of ½ lemon
2–3 drops green jalapeño hot sauce
pinch of salt

To make the fritters, place the corn, flour, flax eggs, spring onions, salt, pepper, parsley and 2 tablespoons of the oil in a bowl. Mix until combined.

Put the remaining oil in a frying pan over medium heat. Spoon about 60 ml (2 fl oz/¼ cup) batter at a time into the pan and cook for 2–3 minutes, then flip and cook for another 2–3 minutes on the other side.

For the smash, place the avocado, cashew 'goat's' cheese, lemon juice, jalapeño hot sauce and salt in a bowl. Mash together with a fork.

Serve the fritters immediately with the smash.

MEDITERRANEAN BAKED BEANS

Serves 2
Prep time: 5 minutes
Cooking time: 15 minutes

'Wow' and 'Yum' are the two most common responses when I serve someone this dish. These baked beans will make you never, ever want to look at another tin of supermarket beans again. These are beyond flavoursome, the smell is beautiful and they are ridiculously easy to make! They will definitely transport you to the Mediterranean, even if it is just for half an hour of your busy morning.

400 g (14 oz) tinned cannellini (lima) beans
2 French shallots, diced
1 tablespoon plant-based oil*
2 garlic cloves, crushed
200 g (7 oz/1 cup) chopped tomatoes
½ teaspoon pink lake salt*
½ teaspoon freshly ground black pepper
½ teaspoon sweet paprika
½ teaspoon sumac
½ teaspoon dried mint
¼ teaspoon ground coriander
130 g (4½ oz/2 cups) chopped English
    spinach, silverbeet (Swiss chard) or kale
½ avocado to serve
30 g (1 oz/½ cup) chopped flat-leaf parsley
    to serve
2 tablespoons hemp seeds* to serve

Rinse and drain the cannellini beans.

In a non-stick saucepan over medium heat, sauté the shallots in the plant-based oil. After they begin to turn translucent, add the garlic and cook for another minute. Next add the beans, tomatoes, salt, pepper, spices and herbs. Let simmer for 10 minutes or until the tomato liquid thickens.

Add the chopped English spinach then remove immediately from the heat.

Serve straight away with the avocado and the parsley and hemp seeds sprinkled on top.

MEXICAN SCRAMBLED TOFU

Serves 2–4
Prep time: 10 minutes
Cooking time: 10 minutes

When I first gave up eggs, one of the biggest things I missed was a traditional scrambled egg breakfast. I tried various alternatives, including scrambled tofu on its own, which isn't very appealing. This dish, however, packs an absolute punch in the morning. The flavours dive around your mouth taking your tastebuds into another world. It's a simple concept but it's just so great. This is by far one of my favourite breakfasts. Being high in protein, your metabolism will get a kick start too!

1 tablespoon plant-based oil*
300 g (10½ oz) firm tofu
1 teaspoon cumin
1 small capsicum (bell pepper), diced
180 g (6½ oz/2 cups) chopped button
    mushrooms
2 tablespoons Turmeric butter (page 224)
1 tinned or dried chipotle chilli* (if dried,
    first soak in water for 20 minutes)
1 splash Simple hot sauce (page 232) or
    Tabasco
½ teaspoon salt
½ teaspoon freshly ground black pepper
2 tablespoons tomato paste (concentrated
    purée)
25 g (1 oz/½ cup) baby English spinach or
    chopped kale
½ avocado, sliced, to serve
¼ bunch coriander (cilantro) leaves,
    chopped, to serve

Put the plant-based oil and crumble the tofu into a medium frying pan over medium heat. Sprinkle over the cumin and mix into the tofu. Add the capsicum, mushrooms, turmeric butter, chipotle chilli, hot sauce, salt, pepper and tomato paste.

Cook for 5–10 minutes until the vegetables are softened and everything is well heated through. Add the spinach, stir through and remove from the heat.

Serve with the avocado and coriander.

APPLE PANCAKES WITH MAPLE CASHEW ICE CREAM

I don't know anyone who can say no to pancakes. They are such a joy to wake up to in the morning and always start the day on a good note. These pancakes are dedicated to my amazing friend Greta as, every time we get breakfast together, neither of us can ever resist the pancake option!

Serves 4
Prep time: 20 minutes, plus soaking time
Cooking time: 15 minutes

Maple cashew ice cream
125 ml (4 fl oz/½ cup) maple syrup
155 g (5½ oz/1 cup) cashews (soaked in water for 3 hours or preferably overnight)
½ teaspoon vanilla extract
¼ teaspoon salt
400 ml (13½ fl oz) tin coconut cream

Apple pancakes
1 green apple, cored
130 g (4½ oz/1 cup) buckwheat flour
105 g (3½ oz/½ cup) stevia*
1 teaspoon baking powder

To serve
155 g (5½ oz/1 cup) fresh blueberries or other berries of your choice
maple syrup to drizzle (optional)

Start by making the ice cream. In a food processor or blender, mix together the maple syrup, cashews, vanilla, salt and coconut cream. Once smooth, churn the mixture in an ice cream maker for 15 minutes or until set. Set aside in the freezer while you cook the pancakes.

For the pancakes, grate the apple into a bowl. Add the buckwheat flour, 170 ml (5½ fl oz/⅔ cup) water, the stevia and baking powder. Mix together to form a thin batter.

Using a ladle or ice cream scoop, place small rounds of the pancake batter in a non-stick frying pan over medium heat. Cook each pancake for about 2 minutes or until it begins to bubble, then flip it over and cook for a further minute on the other side before removing from the pan. Continue until all the batter is used up (the batter will make about 8 pancakes).

To serve, place the pancakes in a stack on each plate, with a scoop of the maple syrup ice cream, a sprinkling of fresh berries and a drizzle of maple syrup, if desired.

MANGO AND COCONUT BREAD WITH POACHED STONE FRUIT

This is inspired by one of my favourite Melbourne cafe breakfasts, which I unfortunately had to give up when I became a vegan. I love making this bread just as much as I love eating it. It fills the house with a beautiful smell and is always a stunning dish to serve up to guests.

Serves 4
Prep time: 5 minutes
Cooking time: 15–20 minutes

Mango and coconut bread
195 g (7 oz/1½ cups) buckwheat flour
1 teaspoon bicarbonate of soda
   (baking soda)
1 teaspoon salt
190 g (6½ oz/1 cup) coconut sugar* or xylitol*
2 flax eggs* ('no egg' replacement mix)
1 teaspoon cinnamon
60 g (2 oz/1 cup) shredded coconut
70 g (2½ oz/½ cup) nuts of choice (optional)
½ teaspoon coconut oil
1 teaspoon vanilla extract
1 teaspoon apple cider vinegar
juice and zest of 1 lime
flesh of 1 mango, puréed, plus 1 large mango
   or 95 g (3¼ oz/½ cup) frozen mango, diced

Poached stone fruit
4 stone fruits of your choice
2 tablespoons coconut syrup

To serve
80 g (2¾ oz) Coconut yoghurt (see page 16)
strawberries (optional)
1 mint sprig
1 tablespoon micro green sprouts

Preheat the oven to 180°C (350°F) and line 1 small loaf (bar) tin or 6 small tins with baking paper.

For the bread, in a bowl mix together the dry ingredients. Add all the wet ingredients, except the diced mango, and stir to combine.

Gently fold in the diced mango and place the mixture into the lined tin/s. Bake in the oven for 15–20 minutes or until a skewer comes out clean.

While the bread is cooking, cut each stone fruit in half and place in a saucepan with 2 tablespoons water and the coconut syrup. Let simmer for 10 minutes or until the stone fruit begins to soften. Remove from the heat and set aside.

Slice the loaf and distribute the slices or mini-loaves between 4 plates. Add 2 stone fruit pieces and serve each bowl with 1 tablespoon coconut yoghurt, strawberries if using, a few mint leaves and 1 teaspoon micro green sprouts.

BANANA CHIA BREAD

Makes 10 slices
Prep time: 10 minutes
Cooking time: 30–45 minutes

Banana bread is always a staple. Walk into any cafe and, if they don't have some banana bread sitting in the counter window, you can be pretty sure they will have it on their menu. Banana bread is also so simple to make. You can cook it, slice it and freeze it for later or just eat it straight away. It's the perfect breakfast comfort food.

160 g (5½ oz/1¼ cups) buckwheat flour
160 (5½ oz/1 cup) brown rice flour
55 g (2 oz/½ cup) ground almonds
2 teaspoons baking powder
80 g (2¾ oz/⅓ cup) coconut sugar*
1 teaspoon bicarbonate of soda
  (baking soda)
30 g (1 oz) flaxmeal*
2 teaspoons cinnamon
1 teaspoon mixed spice
½ teaspoon salt
50 g (1¾ oz/½ cup) walnuts
30 g (1 oz/¼ cup) chia seeds*
60 ml (2 fl oz/¼ cup) plant-based milk*,
  plus extra 2 tablespoons
3 large overripe bananas, plus 1 ripe banana
125 ml (4 fl oz/½ cup) water
80 ml (2½ fl oz/⅓ cup) maple syrup
60 ml (2 fl oz/¼ cup) plant-based oil*
2 teaspoons vanilla extract

Preheat the oven to 180°C (350°F). Grease a 10 × 7.5 cm (4 × 3 in) loaf (bar) tin and line it with baking paper.

Place all the dry ingredients, except the chia seeds, in a mixing bowl and stir to combine.

Soak the chia seeds for 10 minutes in the 2 extra tablespoons milk.

In a bowl, mash the 3 overripe bananas until smooth. Add, along with the other liquid ingredients, including the chia seeds, to the dry ingredients and stir to combine with a wooden spoon. Once combined, transfer to the lined tin. Slice the remaining banana in half lengthways and place it on top of the mixture in the tin. Bake in the oven for 30–45 minutes or until a metal skewer comes out clean. Let the banana bread cool completely in the tin before you take it out and slice it, to avoid the bread falling apart.

Spread with coconut oil or the nut butter of your choice and enjoy. If eating it after the first day, lightly grill (broil) the banana bread. Store in an airtight container for up to 3 days or slice and place in individual plastic bags to freeze.

FRENCH TOAST WAFFLES WITH BERRY COMPOTE

It's safe to say this is one of my favourite breakfasts – ever. Not only is this recipe super-easy to make, it is so delicious, wholesome and you will be filled up for hours. No more super-rich stodgy French toast, leaving you feeling like a slug. This healthy version is light, fresh and will have your tummy feeling nourished and happy!

Serves 4
Prep time: 5 minutes
Cooking time: 40 minutes

175 g (6 oz) Macadamia 'ricotta' cheese
  (page 223)
1 lime (quartered)

Waffles
130 g (4½ oz/1 cup) buckwheat flour
1 teaspoon baking powder
1 tablespoon stevia*
250 ml (8½ fl oz/1 cup) plant-based milk*
60 ml (2 fl oz/¼ cup) maple syrup

French toast mix
400 ml (13½ fl oz) tin coconut cream
60 ml (2 fl oz/¼ cup) plant-based milk*
60 ml (2 fl oz/¼ cup) maple syrup

Berry compote
155 g (5½ oz/1 cup) mixed berries
3 teaspoons stevia*

For the waffles, combine the buckwheat flour, baking powder and stevia in a bowl. Whisk in the milk and maple syrup.

Depending on the size of your waffle maker, place a quarter or an eighth of the mixture in the waffle iron. Cook until the outside is golden (around 3–5 minutes) and remove.

For the French toast mix, in a bowl combine the coconut cream, milk and maple syrup. Mix until combined.

Heat a medium frying pan over high heat until hot. Dunk each waffle into the French toast mix and then place in the pan, cooking the waffles one at a time, until golden on the outside.

For the compote, combine the berries, 60 ml (2 fl oz/¼ cup) water and the stevia in a saucepan over medium heat and let simmer until the liquid reduces and begins to thicken.

To serve, place 1–2 waffles on each plate, top with the berry compote and 1 tablespoon of the macadamia 'ricotta'. Serve immediately with a lime wedge on each plate.

HAZELNUT AND CACAO BROWN RICE CRISPS

Serves 4
Prep time: 10 minutes
Cooking time: 10 minutes

This recipe was donated to the book by my Californian friend Diem Ly Vo. I met Diem while I was in San Jose and was blown away by her talent, her knowledge and her amazing inner beauty. Diem specialises in vegan and macrobiotic foods and is truly outstanding in her flavour combinations. I was lucky enough to get to cook with her in the kitchen and eat her food, and I am longing for the time we get to do it again. This is her take on the classic breakfast cereal Coco Pops/ Krispies. There is always a jar of this in my pantry now!

2 tablespoons coconut oil
30 g (1 oz) hazelnut butter
¼ teaspoon vanilla extract
2 tablespoons cacao powder*
1 tablespoon maple syrup
pinch of pink lake salt*
60 g (2 oz/2 cups) plain brown rice crisps*
plant-based milk* to serve
berries to serve (optional)

Preheat the oven to 180°C (350°F).

Over a double boiler, combine the coconut oil, hazelnut butter, vanilla, cacao, maple syrup and salt. Once the oil and butter have melted and the mixture is well combined, set the bowl aside.

Place the brown rice crisps on a baking tray lined with baking paper. Pour the cacao mixture over the crisps and use a spoon or spatula to evenly coat the crisps.

Bake for 10 minutes, mixing and redistributing half-way through.

Serve with a plant-based milk and berries or however you like. Store in an airtight jar for up to 1 month.

MORNING FRUIT GALETTE

Galettes have got to be one of the prettiest breakfasts around. A galette is such a simple dish with pastry and fruit, yet there is something so divine about it! These galettes are brilliant to make and put on the table to cut up and nibble on when you have guests, or to devour on your own.

Serves 2–4
Prep time: 15 minutes
Cooking time: 25 minutes

Pastry
130 g (4½ oz/1 cup) buckwheat flour
90 g (3 oz/½ cup) brown rice flour
1 tablespoon stevia*
¼ teaspoon pink lake salt*
½ teaspoon baking powder
125 g (4½ oz/½ cup) vegan plant-based spread or coconut butter

Fruit
2 peaches
2 nectarines
handful blueberries
2 tablespoons coconut nectar*
½ teaspoon vanilla extract

To serve
vegan yoghurt

Preheat the oven to 180°C (350°F).

For the pastry, mix the flours, stevia, salt and baking powder in a bowl. Add the vegan spread and rub it in with your fingertips until the mixture is a coarse breadcrumb texture.

Add 190 ml (6½ fl oz/¾ cup) water and gently mix to form a dough, adding more water if necessary.

Roll out on a floured surface and, with a cutter or by hand, form into rough flat circles, about 7.5 cm (3 in) in diameter, then set aside.

For the fruit, cut the peaches and nectarines into slices and place in a small saucepan over medium heat with the blueberries, coconut nectar, vanilla and 2 tablespoons water. Let simmer for 2–3 minutes until the stone fruit just begins to soften and the liquid has reduced.

Remove the stone fruit from the pan and arrange on the middle of the pastry circles. Top the fruit with extra coconut nectar if desired.

Fold the pastry circles in around the edges and place in the oven for 20 minutes or until golden. Serve the galettes immediately with yoghurt.

POP TARTS

Makes 9–12
Prep time: 30 minutes, plus 2 hours resting
Cooking time: 15 minutes

260 g (9 oz/2 cups) buckwheat flour
45 g (1½ oz) coconut sugar*
½ teaspoon salt
¼ teaspoon baking powder
125 g (4½ oz) vegan butter
60 ml (2 fl oz/¼ cup) plant-based milk*
1 tablespoon flaxmeal*
150 g (5½ oz) Chocolate hazelnut butter
  (page 227)
125 g (4½ oz) Berry chia jam (page 219)

Vanilla icing
2 tablespoons stevia*
1 teaspoon cornflour (cornstarch)
1 teaspoon vanilla extract
1 tablespoon maple syrup

Chocolate icing
2 tablespoons Chocolate hazelnut butter
  (page 227)

This recipe is inspired by my trip to the United States and the huge array of breakfast toaster pastries that were available there. Having to restrain myself from the super-processed and sugar-packed treats, I decided there needed to be a healthier version and came up with this recipe that everyone and anyone can easily make at home. I cannot emphasise the praise I get when I make this recipe. It will turn any health food-wary person into a health food enthusiast!

In a food processor, combine the buckwheat flour, coconut sugar, salt and baking powder. Slowly add the vegan butter and then the plant-based milk, flaxmeal and 2 tablespoons water. Once a dough forms, remove it from the food processor, wrap in plastic wrap and place in the refrigerator for 2 hours.

Remove half of the dough from the refrigerator, roll out on a well-floured surface and cut into desired shapes – I either use rectangles or circles. Place 1 tablespoon of either chocolate hazelnut butter or jam onto each cut-out.

Preheat the oven to 180°C (350°F).

Remove the second half of the dough from the refrigerator, roll out and cut into exactly the same shapes as before. Place the shapes on top of the others and press down the edges with a fork to seal. Prick the tops with a fork and then bake in the oven for 15 minutes until golden.

For the vanilla icing, mix the stevia, cornflour, vanilla and maple syrup in a bowl. Drizzle over the pop tarts filled with raspberry jam.

For the chocolate icing, gently heat the hazelnut butter in a double boiler until melted and then drizzle over the chocolate hazelnut-filled pop tarts.

Enjoy immediately or store in an airtight container for up to a week.

LUNCH

Mornings can be busy and mentally strenuous. Lunch is the time of day that I stop, breathe and recoup. However, sometimes I don't have lunch until about 3 or 4 as I just keep going and seem to forget the time. Sometimes lunch is a shambles – something I put together using leftovers from the night before, or that I made quickly at 6 am that morning, knowing I won't have time to make lunch. However, other times lunch is slow. I cook slowly, I think about what I am making and how all the ingredients are working together. I give myself time to sit outside, feel the sun on my face, enjoy the beautiful outdoors and be still. I savour each mouthful and concentrate on each bite and my chewing. It's like meditation. I let my mind wander, I only focus on what's on the plate or bowl in front of me, and I enjoy all the flavours and fresh ingredients.

If I don't stop for lunch, later that day I find myself in a slump, feeling like a disorientated slug, not sure what I'm doing. My mind has too many things built up and I can't focus on the task in front of me.

Give yourself time for lunch, even if it's just 15 minutes. Clear some of those thoughts from your mind – plan, enjoy and breathe.

These recipes are all simple and quick. If you haven't put them together the night before, they take no time to whip up when you do have a moment to stop and breathe.

ARTICHOKE, WHITE BEAN AND LEMON
TOASTED SANDWICHES 49

BROCCOLI FRITTERS 50

CAULIFLOWER AND BROCCOLI SOUP
WITH SWEET POTATO CRISPS 53

FENNEL, ORANGE AND
ROCKET SALAD 54

GRILLED SQUASH AND PEACH
SUMMER SALAD 57

KING OYSTER 'SCALLOP' AND
ROCKET FETTUCCINE 58

ROASTED PEAR AND LENTIL
SALAD 61

PUMPKIN AND SWEET POTATO
EMPANADAS 62

ROASTED VEGETABLE SALAD WITH
CASHEW 'GOAT'S' CHEESE 65

GREEN GARDEN MINESTRONE 66

THE STAPLE SALAD 69

ZUCCHINI AND MINT
BRUSCHETTA 70

ARTICHOKE, WHITE BEAN AND LEMON TOASTED SANDWICHES

I first had this sandwich many years ago over a long lunch with an old friend and my mum. The sandwich completely summed up our mood – light, happy and healthy, yet still with a hint of naughtiness. You won't often catch me eating a sandwich but, when I do, you can almost bet that it will be this one!

Serves 4
Prep time: 10 minutes
Cooking time: 12 minutes

1 tablespoon plant-based oil*
2 garlic cloves, crushed
400 g (14 oz) tinned artichoke hearts, drained and rinsed
400 g (14 oz) tinned cannellini (lima) beans, drained and rinsed, or dried beans soaked for 18 hours in water
zest and juice of 1 lemon, plus extra to serve
1 teaspoon salt
½ teaspoon freshly ground black pepper
8 slices gluten-free bread
40 g (1½ oz) Cashew 'goat's' cheese (page 220)
1 tablespoon vegan mayonnaise
60 g (2 oz/1 cup) snow pea sprouts
lemon wedge to serve

Heat the plant-based oil in a small frying pan over medium heat. Add the garlic and cook for 1 minute. Add the artichoke hearts and cannellini beans. Using a masher, very lightly press down to lightly smash but not mash the ingredients. Add the lemon zest and juice, salt and pepper and let the mixture heat up for 3–5 minutes.

Place 4 slices of the gluten-free bread in a sandwich press. Spread on 1 tablespoon of the cashew 'goat's' cheese (or you can serve this on the side), 1 teaspoon of the vegan mayonnaise, a quarter of the sprouts and some extra lemon zest on each slice.

Divide the bean and artichoke mixture onto each of the slices and top with the remaining bread slices. Let the sandwiches cook for 5 minutes until golden. Serve with a wedge of lemon.

BROCCOLI FRITTERS

Fritters are such a great lunch and you can eat them on their own or with salad. These delicious broccoli fritters are simple, tasty and are filled with heaps of nutrients to keep you fuelled up until dinner.

Serves 3–4
Prep time: 10 minutes
Cooking time: 15 minutes

Broccoli fritters
½ head broccoli, chopped into very
   small pieces
65 g (2¼ oz/½ cup) buckwheat flour
2 tablespoons flaxmeal*
80 ml (2½ fl oz/⅓ cup) water
½ red onion, diced
½ teaspoon salt
½ teaspoon freshly ground black pepper
1 tablespoon savoury yeast flakes*
90 g (3 oz/⅓ cup) Cashew 'goat's' cheese
   (page 220) or Macadamia 'ricotta' cheese
   (page 223)
2 tablespoons plant-based oil*
1 tablespoon chopped flat-leaf parsley

To serve
lemon wedges
125 g (4½ oz/½ cup) vegan yoghurt

Steam the broccoli for 2–3 minutes. Remove from the heat and set aside.

In a bowl, mix the remaining ingredients, then add the broccoli. Form the mixture into palm-sized patties and place in a non-stick frying pan over medium heat and cook for 5 minutes on each side.

Serve the fritters with the lemon wedges and yoghurt. Store in the refrigerator for up to 2 days.

CAULIFLOWER AND BROCCOLI SOUP WITH SWEET POTATO CRISPS

This is one of the most comforting soups. As soon as the weather begins to shift from summer into cool autumn, I have a pot of this ready on the stove. It's so simple, creamy and delicious. It's an absolute favourite for me to make and pop in a thermos for my weekly lunch. When paired with the delicious sweet potato crisps, it's a match made in heaven! This soup is almost too easy to make. All you need is a steamer, a blender, a saucepan and your oven switched on.

Serves 4
Prep time: 10 minutes
Cooking time: 20 minutes

Sweet potato crisps
1 large sweet potato
1 tablespoon coconut oil
salt
freshly ground black pepper

Cauliflower and broccoli soup
1 head cauliflower
1 head broccoli
1 brown onion, chopped
2 leeks, chopped
3 garlic cloves, crushed
splash of olive oil, plus extra for drizzling
1 litre (34 fl oz/4 cups) low-sodium vegetable or faux chicken stock
1 teaspoon dried thyme
½ teaspoon dried marjoram
pinch of chilli flakes
35 g (1¼ oz/⅓ cup) grated cheese, such as parmesan, or 20 g (¾ oz) savoury yeast flakes* if vegan
60 ml (2 fl oz/¼ cup) coconut cream
salt
freshly ground black pepper
flat-leaf parsley to garnish

Preheat the oven to 180°C (350°F) and line a baking tray with baking paper.

For the crisps, slice the sweet potato into very thin slices using a mandoline. Put the slices in a bowl with the coconut oil, season to taste and toss until coated. Place the sweet potato evenly on the baking tray and pop them in the oven. After 10 minutes, flip them over to cook the other side. Bake for another 5 minutes until crisp then remove from the oven and set aside.

For the soup, break up your heads of broccoli and cauliflower and steam them for 5 minutes.

Meanwhile, put the onion, leek and garlic in a saucepan over medium heat and sauté in the olive oil until translucent. Transfer the mixture to a blender with half the stock. Blitz until smooth and pour back into the soup pan.

Place the steamed cauliflower and broccoli in the blender with the remaining stock and blitz again until silky smooth. Pour this into the soup pan with the onion and leek mixture and stir. Add the herbs, chilli flakes, cheese and coconut cream and season with salt and pepper. Serve with a drizzle of olive oil, a sprinkle of black pepper, some chopped parsley and the sweet potato chips. Store the soup in a container in the refrigerator for up to 3 days or freeze for up to 3 months.

FENNEL, ORANGE AND ROCKET SALAD

This salad always reminds me of sunshine. The colours are so vibrant and it just lights up the plate. It's perfect to serve at a barbecue to bring a rainbow of colour to the table, or to bring a spot of sunshine to any lunchbreak.

Serves 2–4
Prep time: 10 minutes

2 oranges
1 bulb fennel
2 tablespoons pepitas (pumpkin seeds)
15 g (½ oz/⅓ cup) rocket (arugula)
2 tablespoons dill, chopped

Dressing
2 tablespoons olive oil
1 tablespoon white wine vinegar
¼ teaspoon wholegrain mustard
1 teaspoon rice malt syrup*
juice of ½ orange
¼ teaspoon salt

Peel the oranges and thinly slice them. Chop the top and bottom off the fennel, discard and then slice the remaining part of the bulb thinly in a similar fashion to the oranges.

Arrange the orange and fennel on a plate with the pepitas, rocket and dill.

Mix all the dressing ingredients together, lightly pour over the salad and serve.

GRILLED SQUASH AND PEACH SUMMER SALAD

This salad is something that I love to make when stone fruit comes into season. It's extremely easy, beautiful in colour and tastes an absolute treat. I enjoy serving it to friends for lunch as each mouthful is so flavoursome and sweet and it's beautiful to present. It almost represents the end of summer – colours like a beautiful sunset and the sweetness of the sun that is just clinging on to ripen the squash and stone fruit.

Serves 2–4
Prep time: 10 minutes
Cooking time: 15 minutes

2 ripe peaches
150 g (5½ oz) mixed summer squash, such as
    baby (pattypan) squash or yellow zucchini
    (courgette)
1 tablespoon plant-based oil*
2 tablespoons chopped mint
1 tablespoon chopped flat-leaf parsley
1 tablespoon chopped basil
2 tablespoons micro herbs

Dressing
1 tablespoon plant-based oil*
1 teaspoon rice malt syrup*
½ teaspoon salt
zest of 1 lime
juice of ½ lime

Slice the peaches and squash into shapes or slices of your choice.

Brush a ridged griddle pan with the plant-based oil, heat over medium–high heat and place the peach and squash on the pan. Grill for 2–3 minutes before flipping and cooking for a further 2–3 minutes. Once done on each side, remove and place on a serving plate.

Sprinkle over the herbs and set aside.

In a separate bowl combine all the dressing ingredients. Pour the dressing onto the salad and serve.

KING OYSTER 'SCALLOP' AND ROCKET FETTUCCINE

The simplicity of this dish is what I love the most. It is so quick and easy to make yet you will feel like you're dining in a fancy restaurant. I was first introduced to the 'scallop' mushroom by a friend in California, and have not been able to resist it ever since. The mushroom slices look deviously like seafood scallops!

Serves 4
Prep time: 5 minutes
Cooking time: 20 minutes

1½ teaspoons salt
400 g (14 oz) gluten-free fettuccine
4 king oyster mushrooms
60 ml (2 fl oz/¼ cup) macadamia oil
½ teaspoon ground kelp
¼ teaspoon freshly ground black pepper
40 g (1½ oz/2 cups) rocket (arugula)
2 tablespoons chopped flat-leaf parsley

Boil 2 litres (68 fl oz/8 cups) water in a medium saucepan and add 1 teaspoon of the salt. Once the water is boiling, add the fettuccine and stir to prevent it from sticking together. Cook the pasta for 8–10 minutes or until tender. Remove from the heat and drain.

Meanwhile, slice each king oyster mushroom stalk into around 5 slices crossways to make 'scalllop' shapes (don't use the top of the mushroom – I like to keep these in the refrigerator and use them for my Mexican scrambled tofu, page 28 or Wild mushroom risotto, page 146).

Heat 2 tablespoons of the macadamia oil in a small saucepan over high heat and evenly place all the 'scallop' pieces in the pan. Season with the kelp, pepper and the remaining salt. Fry each side of the scallops for 5 minutes until golden.

Divide the rocket between 4 plates.

Toss the pasta in the remaining macadamia oil and divide among the plates with the rocket. Add 5 scallop pieces to each plate and top with parsley. Drizzle over extra macadamia oil if desired and serve immediately.

ROASTED PEAR AND LENTIL SALAD

This salad is simple and delicious. It's easy to make, contains heaps of nutrients to fuel you and has lots of different textures to ensure maximum satisfaction. The sweetness of the roasted pear goes perfectly with the slight tartness of the hibiscus vinegar and creates an amazing flavour sensation in your mouth.

Serves 2–4
Prep time: 10 minutes
Cooking time: 15 minutes

2 pears
2 tablespoons rice malt syrup*
¾ teaspoon salt
1 teaspoon plant-based oil*
400 g (14 oz) tinned brown lentils
2 tablespoons pepitas (pumpkin seeds)
1 tablespoon sunflower seeds
80 g (2¾ oz/2 cups) mixed salad leaves
2 tablespoons orange juice
1 teaspoon hibiscus vinegar*
1 tablespoon olive oil

Preheat the oven to 180°C (350°F).

Slice the pears and place them in a bowl with the rice malt syrup, ¼ teaspoon of the salt and the plant-based oil. Toss everything together to coat the pears.

Place the pears on a baking tray and bake in the oven for 15 minutes until nicely roasted.

Drain and rinse the lentils and place them in a bowl with the pepitas, sunflower seeds, remaining salt and mixed salad leaves. Mix together and place in 2 to 4 serving bowls or plates. Top with the roasted pears.

In a small bowl combine the orange juice, hibiscus vinegar and olive oil and lightly drizzle this dressing over the salad at the last minute before serving.

PUMPKIN AND SWEET POTATO EMPANADAS

Makes 24 empanadas
Prep time: 15 minutes
Cooking time: 45 minutes

I have to give credit to my mum for this recipe. The first time she made these my tastebuds exploded. I knew they had to be in the book. Inspired by our trip to Argentina, these little pocket-sized babies are perfect for on-the-go lunches or for serving to guests or family. They are beyond tasty and it's hard to stop at just one! You can also pop them in the freezer, ready to reheat in the oven anytime.

800 g (1 lb 12 oz) pumpkin (winter squash)
300 g (10½ oz) sweet potato
1 large red onion, diced
2 tablespoons plant-based oil*
¼ teaspoon nutmeg
⅛ teaspoon ground cloves
¼ teaspoon chilli flakes
½ teaspoon cinnamon
¼ teaspoon paprika
salt
freshly ground black pepper
6 sheets gluten-free puff pastry*

Peel the pumpkin and sweet potato, chop into small pieces and steam for 10–15 minutes. Once tender, remove from the steamer and set aside.

Meanwhile, in a medium frying pan over medium heat, cook the onion in the plant-based oil until caramelised, 5–10 minutes.

In a bowl, mix the vegetables, the onion mixture, spices and season with salt and pepper.

Preheat the oven to 180°C (350°F).

Cut each pastry sheet into 4. Using a 10 cm (4 in) round cutter, cut a round out of each piece of pastry (or use an empanada press and cutter, if you have one). Place 2 tablespoons filling on one side of each pastry sheet. Fold over the pastry and press the edges together with a fork to seal.

Bake the empanadas in the oven for 20–30 minutes until golden brown. Serve immediately.

Store in the refrigerator in an airtight container for up to 3–4 days or freeze for up to 3 months.

ROASTED VEGETABLE SALAD WITH CASHEW 'GOAT'S' CHEESE

This is by far my favourite easy salad. It takes no time to prepare, it's vibrant and it's delicious. A lot of people shrug salads off as being boring or not filling enough – and, as Homer Simpson says, 'you don't win friends with salad'. However, this salad definitely proves them wrong. It is a meal in itself, it's so versatile and you feel good eating it.

Serves 4
Prep time: 10 minutes
Cooking time: 30 minutes

½ cauliflower, cut into bite-sized pieces
½ large sweet potato, cut into bite-sized pieces
¼ pumpkin (winter squash), cut into bite-sized pieces
2 teaspoons turmeric
2 teaspoons cumin seeds
1 teaspoon cinnamon
½ teaspoon cayenne pepper
pinch of salt
pinch of freshly ground black pepper
60 ml (2 fl oz/¼ cup) coconut oil, melted
2 fresh beetroots (beets), cut into bite-sized pieces
½ bunch kale
olive oil to drizzle
30 g (1 oz/¼ cup) Cashew 'goat's' cheese (page 220), or any vegan cashew cheese, crumbled
60 g (2 oz/¼ cup) sprouts of your choice
30 g (1 oz/¼ cup) chopped walnuts

Preheat the oven to 180°C (350°F).

Place the vegetables, except the beetroot and kale, in a mixing bowl and coat with the spices, seasoning and coconut oil and mix until everything is combined. Transfer the vegetables to a baking tray, but don't clean the bowl yet.

Add the beetroot to the bowl and cover with all the remaining spices and oil left in the bowl and then place on the tray with the rest of the vegetables. (We do the beetroot separately as otherwise all the vegetables end up purple!)

Bake the vegetables for 20–30 minutes until soft inside but crunchy on the outside. You may need to turn them half-way through.

While the vegetables are baking, chop the kale, place it in a large bowl and drizzle with olive oil. Massage the leaves of the kale until they are covered with the olive oil.

Once the vegetables are done place them in the bowl with the kale and lightly toss, being careful not to mush up the sweet potato and pumpkin.

Top the salad with the crumbled cashew 'goat's' cheese, sprouts and chopped walnuts and you're ready to serve.

GREEN GARDEN MINESTRONE

Serves 4
Prep time: 5 minutes
Cooking time: 30 minutes

Anything even slightly Italian makes me happy. When I eat this soup I feel as if I am in the Italian countryside, rugged up in something warm. I like to make this if I am feeling under the weather or think I have a cold coming on, because the soup is filled with healthy green vegetables.

1 leek, sliced
3 garlic cloves, crushed
1 teaspoon dried marjoram
½ teaspoon dried thyme
2 tablespoons plant-based oil*
2 bunches asparagus, chopped
1 bunch broccolini, chopped
95 g (3¼ oz/½ cup) broad (fava) beans
1 litre (34 fl oz/4 cups) low-sodium faux
   chicken stock
400 g (14 oz) tinned artichoke hearts,
   drained, rinsed and quartered
80 g (2¾ oz/½ cup) frozen peas
zest and juice of 1 lemon
½ teaspoon salt
½ teaspoon freshly ground black pepper
15 g (½ oz/¼ cup) chopped mint
7 g (¼ oz/¼ cup) chopped flat-leaf parsley
crunchy bread to serve

Cook the leek, garlic, marjoram and thyme in the plant-based oil in a large saucepan over medium heat for around 5 minutes or until the leek begins to turn translucent.

Add the asparagus, broccolini, broad beans, stock and artichoke hearts and cook for 10 minutes and then add the peas, lemon zest, salt and pepper.

Cook for another 5 minutes then add the chopped mint and parsley and check the seasoning again.

Serve topped with a squeeze of lemon juice in each bowl and a good hunk of crunchy bread.

THE STAPLE SALAD

Serves 2–4
Prep time: 5 minutes
Cooking time: 10 minutes

This salad is inspired by my old boss; someone who took me under her wing, always gave me health advice and wowed me with her beautiful foods. That lady is Catherine Gett of The Staple Store and A Staple Space in Melbourne, Australia, where I live. I always think of Catie when I make this salad. It's so beautifully delicious and yet so simple to make.

1 bunch broccolini, cut into thirds
4 large kale leaves, chopped
400 g (14 oz) tinned chickpeas (garbanzo beans), drained and rinsed
30 g (1 oz) crushed toasted almonds
60 g (2 oz) dried cranberries
45 g (1½ oz) pine nuts
1 tablespoon pepitas (pumpkin seeds)
1 tablespoon black sesame seeds
1 tablespoon sunflower seeds
2 tablespoons olive oil, plus extra for drizzling
1 tablespoon pomegranate vinegar*
½ tablespoon pomegranate molasses
½ teaspoon salt
½ teaspoon freshly ground black pepper
juice of ½ lemon

Blanch the broccolini and kale for 2 minutes in a bowl of boiling water, remove and place in a bowl with the chickpeas, almonds and cranberries.

In a small frying pan on low, gently heat the pine nuts, pepitas, sesame seeds and sunflower seeds until golden, about 2 minutes. Add to the salad and toss.

In a small bowl, mix the olive oil, pomegranate vinegar, pomegranate molasses, salt, pepper and lemon juice. Stir to combine, dress the salad and serve. Drizzle over some extra olive oil, if desired.

ZUCCHINI AND MINT BRUSCHETTA

This really is a 10-minute lunch. When I am absolutely on a deadline and my brain can't even think about what to make, this is my go-to dish. Even the most kitchen-shy person can make this and enjoy a nourishing, filling and flavoursome lunch.

Serves 1–2
Prep time: 5 minutes
Cooking time: 5 minutes

1 zucchini (courgette)
2 tablespoons chopped fresh mint
¼ teaspoon salt
⅛ teaspoon freshly ground black pepper
¼ teaspoon kelp
zest of 1 lemon
juice of ½ lemon
3 teaspoons olive oil
2 slices good-quality gluten-free baguette
   or ciabatta
1 garlic clove, cut in half
2 tablespoons Cashew 'goat's' cheese
   (page 220)

Start by peeling long ribbon pieces of the zucchini. Place the zucchini pieces in a bowl and add the mint, salt, pepper, kelp, lemon zest, lemon juice and 1 teaspoon of the olive oil. Mix to combine then set aside.

Brush 1 teaspoon of olive oil on each slice of bread. Place under a grill (broiler) until golden, turning half-way through.

Remove from the oven and rub the cut garlic clove on each slice of toasted bread.

Spread each slice of bread with 1 tablespoon of the cashew 'goat's' cheese and then top with the zucchini salad. Serve and enjoy!

SNACKS

Snacking is a part of who I am. I graze constantly, whether it's a cracker with hummus and a bit of fermented veg, a cookie or a bliss ball. I find myself needing a snack every couple of hours to keep my energy levels high. Being constantly in the kitchen also doesn't help my need to snack! The only time I find myself reaching for the dark chocolate-covered almonds or something naughty is if I don't have my usual healthy stock supply in jars on the kitchen pantry shelves. I constantly need to have something to do, whether it be cooking, writing, blogging, jogging, swimming or walking the dogs. I find it very hard to be still. So snacks are of the utmost importance to me. They are the fuel to my fire.

The recipes in this section are some of my favourite go-to snacks; things I make on the weekend to keep on hand to nibble throughout the week.

JALAPEÑO AND GARLIC SWEET POTATO FRIES

When I was in the USA I was introduced to sweet potato fries. To me it was so logical that the sweet potato fry should be served everywhere alongside normal fries. I fell well and truly in love. Although I had made basic sweet potato fries at home, I hadn't yet tried this version and hadn't quite developed my appreciation for the dish. These fries have the best flavour, and are the perfect accompaniment to any meal, or on their own as a little snack!

Serves 2
Prep time: 10 minutes
Cooking time: 20–30 minutes

*1 large sweet potato
1 tablespoon plant-based oil*
¼ teaspoon kelp
½ teaspoon salt
2 garlic cloves, crushed
1–2 jalapeños, sliced
vegan mayonnaise
lime wedges*

Preheat the oven to 180°C (350°F) and line a baking tray with baking paper.

Cut the sweet potato into squared long fry shapes (do not cut too small, as they will shrink in the oven) and place them in a bowl with the plant-based oil, kelp, salt, garlic and jalapeño. Toss together and then spread out evenly on the baking tray.

Cook for 20–30 minutes or until the fries are nice and golden.

Serve with vegan mayonnaise and lime wedges and enjoy!

TOP TO BOTTOM:
MAPLE BEETROOT
HUMMUS, ARTICHOKE
TAHINI HUMMUS,
PARSNIP AND
CORIANDER HUMMUS,
TURMERIC FLAXSEED
CRACKERS

HUMMUS 3 WAYS

Each recipe serves 4
Prep time: 20 minutes
Cooking time: 20 minutes

Hummus is something I have to make weekly (if not twice weekly) and has to be on hand when I need a snack. Hummus is so versatile. It's the perfect dip to have with crackers and chopped-up vegetables. You can also use it on roast vegetables, vegetable patties, or just dolloped on a salad. Not a day goes by where I don't have hummus of some sort. Here are three different variations, each of which has a distinctly delicious flavour.

ARTICHOKE TAHINI HUMMUS

1 leek, sliced
1 tablespoon plant-based oil*
400 g (14 oz) tinned artichoke hearts,
*   drained and rinsed*
2½ tablespoons tahini
200 g (7 oz) tinned chickpeas
*   (garbanzo beans), drained and rinsed*
½ green chilli
2 garlic cloves
80 ml (2½ fl oz/⅓ cup) lemon juice
zest of 1 lemon
½ teaspoon cumin
100 ml (3½ fl oz) olive oil
¼ teaspoon salt
pinch of freshly ground black pepper
1 tablespoon dukkah

Begin by caramelising the leek in the plant-based oil in a frying pan over medium heat for 5 minutes.

Transfer the leek to a food processor with the remaining hummus ingredients, except the dukkah, and blitz until smooth, adding more oil as needed.

Place in a container in the refrigerator. Sprinkle with dukkah just before serving. Store in a jar or airtight container for up to 1 week.

>

PARSNIP AND CORIANDER HUMMUS

3 parsnips, roughly chopped
¼ bunch coriander (cilantro)
200 g (7 oz) tinned chickpeas
   (garbanzo beans), drained and rinsed
2 garlic cloves
60 ml (2 fl oz/¼ cup) olive oil
2 tablespoons lemon juice
1 tablespoon tahini
pinch of salt
1 teaspoon coriander (cilantro) leaves,
   chopped
1 teaspoon coriander seeds

Steam the parsnips until soft, about
10 minutes. Transfer to a food processor and
purée. Add the remaining ingredients, except
the coriander seeds, and blitz until smooth,
adding more oil as needed.

Place in a container in the refrigerator.
Sprinkle with coriander seeds just
before serving. Store in a jar or airtight
container for up to 1 week.

MAPLE BEETROOT HUMMUS

1 beetroot (beet), quartered
½ tablespoon maple syrup
400 g (14 oz) tinned chickpeas
   (garbanzo beans), drained and rinsed
2 tablespoons tahini
juice of 1 lemon
2 garlic cloves
60 ml (2 fl oz/¼ cup) olive oil
¼ teaspoon salt
pinch of freshly ground black pepper
1 tablespoon crushed almonds

Steam the beetroot for about 10 minutes
until tender. Transfer to a food processor
and purée with the maple syrup. Add the
remaining ingredients, except the crushed
almonds, and blitz until smooth, adding more
oil as needed.

Place in a container in the refrigerator.
Sprinkle with the crushed almonds just
before serving. Store in a jar or airtight
container for up to 1 week.

TURMERIC FLAXSEED CRACKERS

Next to the Seaweed sesame crackers (page 87), these crackers are always on hand in my household. I love eating one with a smear of avocado, hummus and lemon. They are extremely crunchy, they are hardly any work to make and are a perfect regular cracker replacement.

Serves 5
Prep time: 10 minutes, plus 1½ hours sitting
Cooking time: 12 hours or overnight

250 g (9 oz/2 cups) flaxseeds*
500 ml (17 fl oz/2 cups) water
1 teaspoon tamari
1 teaspoon turmeric
½ teaspoon salt

Mix all the ingredients in a bowl then cover and let sit for 1½ hours.

Preheat the oven to 75°C (167°F). Line a baking tray with baking paper.

Transfer the mixture from the bowl to the lined baking tray. Spread the mixture out evenly, about 5 mm (¼ in) thick. Make knife ridges in the mixture to mark out the sizes you want your crackers to be. Place in the oven for 12 hours or overnight.

Once removed from the oven you should be able to break the flaxseed crackers into the shapes you marked out. Store in a jar for up to 1 month.

SWEET POTATO ARANCINI BALLS

These are such an excellent snack to grab when you're busy. If I am working hard and just need a little something, I love to eat these as a snack or mini meal! They are delicious and packed with protein and goodness to fill you up and leave you energised.

Makes 24 balls
Prep time: 20 minutes
Cooking time: 35 minutes

220 g (8 oz/1 cup) brown rice
1 sweet potato, chopped
90 g (3 oz/⅓ cup) Macadamia 'ricotta' cheese (page 223)
½ teaspoon salt
½ teaspoon kelp
¼ teaspoon freshly ground black pepper
½ teaspoon dried marjoram
¼ teaspoon dried thyme
50 g (1¾ oz/½ cup) gluten-free dry breadcrumbs

Bring a large saucepan of water to the boil over medium heat. Add the rice and cook until tender, about 15 minutes. Remove from the heat, strain and set aside.

Steam the sweet potato until soft, about 15 minutes. Once steamed, remove from the heat and place in a bowl.

Preheat the oven to 180°C (350°F) and line a baking tray with baking paper.

Mash the sweet potato and then mix in the rice, macadamia 'ricotta', seasonings and herbs.

Roll the mixture into twenty-four 5 cm (2 in) balls. Roll the balls in the breadcrumbs and place on the baking tray. Cook for 20 minutes or until crisp and golden on the outside.

Either serve immediately, or let cool and place in containers. You can store these in the refrigerator, or freeze them for up to 1 month for reheating later.

MUSHROOM PÂTÉ WITH CRISPY BREADSTICKS

Although I have never tried real duck pâté in my life, I imagine this is pretty darn close. My meat-loving dad was fooled and actually believed it was duck pâté and his response was good enough for me! This has a beautiful texture, is high in fibre, potassium and iron – not to mention delicious! The crispy breadsticks are the perfect accompaniment to have with the mushroom pâté, or any dip of choice, and are brilliant to serve to guests.

Serves 4
Prep time: 10 minutes
Cooking time: 30 minutes

Mushroom pâté

3 French shallots, finely sliced
60 ml (2 fl oz/¼ cup) plant-based oil*
2 garlic cloves, crushed
500 g (1 lb 2 oz) button mushrooms, chopped
100 g (3½ oz) tinned chestnuts, drained and rinsed
1 tablespoon tahini
400 g (14 oz) tinned chickpeas (garbanzo beans), drained and rinsed
1 tarragon sprig, finely chopped
½ teaspoon salt
½ teaspoon freshly ground black pepper

Breadsticks

280 g (10 oz) gluten-free bread flour
3½ teaspoons baking powder
1 teaspoon salt
1 teaspoon coconut sugar*
230 ml (8 fl oz) plant-based milk*
30 g (1 oz) vegan butter
50 ml (1¾ fl oz) olive oil
1 tablespoon nigella seeds, sesame seeds or dukkah

For the pâté, sauté the shallots in the oil in a frying pan over medium heat until almost translucent. Add the garlic and cook gently for 2 minutes. Add the mushrooms and cook for 5 minutes.

Put the chestnuts, tahini and chickpeas in a food processor and pulse a couple of times. Add the mushroom mixture and process until smooth. Add the tarragon, salt and pepper.

Place the pâté in a plastic or glass container and press down with a spatula, levelling out the top. Place in the refrigerator until ready to use. (This keeps for a few days in the refrigerator.)

Preheat the oven to 180°C (350°F).

For the breadsticks, mix the flour, baking powder, salt and sugar in a bowl and make a well in the centre. Pour in the milk and mix to a fairly stiff dough. Divide the mixture into 12 and roll each piece into long cylinders.

Place the butter and olive oil in an ovenproof dish and heat in the oven for a couple of minutes to melt the butter. Roll the breadsticks in the butter and oil. Sprinkle with seeds or dukkah, or make a few of each. Bake for 15–20 minutes until golden brown. Serve the pâté with the breadsticks. Store the breadsticks in an airtight container for 2–3 days.

SEAWEED SESAME CRACKERS

I can't live without these crackers. They are super-healthy, very easy to make and make the perfect snack or little something to serve with dips and cheeses – and they look awesome too!

Serves 4
Prep time: 15 minutes, plus sitting
Cooking time: 20–30 minutes

100 g (3½ oz/¾ cup) light buckwheat flour
55 g (2 oz/½ cup) ground almonds
½ teaspoon salt
10 g (¼ oz/¼ cup) dried wakame seaweed*, powdered or in strips
1 sheet nori*, roughly sliced
40 g (1½ oz/¼ cup) sesame seeds

Mix the flour, almonds, salt, wakame and nori in a food processor. Pulse until the seaweed is finely chopped.

Transfer to a bowl and stir in the sesame seeds. Add 80–125 ml (2½–4 fl oz/⅓–½ cup) water and knead into a dough.

Cover and let sit for 10 minutes.

Preheat the oven to 180°C (350°F).

Place the mixture between 2 sheets of baking paper. Roll it out very thinly with a rolling pin. Place on a baking tray and remove the top piece of baking paper.

Cut into squares, rectangles or whatever shapes you like. I prick the crackers with a fork so they don't puff up too much. Bake for 20–30 minutes.

Remove the crackers from the oven, allow to cool and place in a jar or airtight container. Store for up to 2 weeks.

SWEET AND SPICY NUTS

Makes about 150 g (5½ oz/1 cup)
Prep time: 10 minutes
Cooking time: 15 minutes

These nuts are sensational! I could sit down and eat the entire jar in one go. They have the perfect balance of sweet and spice, and are brilliant to serve as a nibble for guests, or to have on hand when you need a little snack fix.

65 g (2¼ oz/⅓ cup) coconut sugar*
1 teaspoon pomegranate molasses
2 tablespoons rice malt syrup*
¼ teaspoon paprika
¼ teaspoon cinnamon
⅛ teaspoon cumin
¼ teaspoon chilli powder
⅛ teaspoon salt
½ teaspoon aleppo pepper*
¼ teaspoon pomegranate seeds
140 g (5 oz/1 cup) mixed nuts of choice

Preheat the oven to 180°C (350°F) and line a baking tray with baking paper.

In a bowl mix together the coconut sugar, pomegranate molasses, rice malt syrup, paprika, cinnamon, cumin, chilli powder, salt, aleppo pepper and pomegranate seeds in a saucepan and warm over low heat for about 5 minutes until the sugar dissolves.

Add the nuts to the saucepan and coat with the mixture.

Pour the nut mixture onto the baking tray and spread it out. Bake in the oven for 10 minutes.

Remove the nuts from the oven and let sit until cooled a little, then peel off the baking paper and allow to cool completely on a non-stick surface.

Once cooled, break the mixture up into nibble-sized pieces. Store in a jar for up to 2 weeks.

RAW GRANOLA BARS

Serves 10–12
Prep time: 10 minutes,
    plus 2–3 hours refrigerating

This is something I often make for my brother to fuel him before he goes on long rides, runs, swims or before a hockey match, as the bars are packed with energy-boosting goodies. These granola bars are easy to put together and are perfect for when you're on the go or just need something to curb your appetite in between meals.

120 g (4½ oz/2 cups) puffed quinoa*
135 g (5 oz/1½ cups) desiccated coconut
45 g (1½ oz/1 cup) puffed amaranth*
360 g (12½ oz/1½ cups) almond butter or
    Almond, brazil and cashew butter (page 227)
190 ml (6½ fl oz/¾ cup) rice malt syrup*
190 g (6½ oz/¾ cup) date paste*
60 ml (2 fl oz/¼ cup) coconut oil
30 g (1 oz/¼ cup) hemp seeds*,
    plus extra for sprinkling
30 g (1 oz/¼ cup) cacao nibs*
2 tablespoons flaxseeds*
2 tablespoons chia seeds*
2 tablespoons sunflower seeds,
    plus extra for sprinkling
pinch of salt

Place all the ingredients in a bowl and mix until combined.

Press the mixture into a lined oven dish or 23 cm (9 in) square brownie tin, sprinkle with a little extra hemp and sunflower seeds and place in the refrigerator to harden, 2–3 hours.

Cut into 10–12 bars. Store in an airtight container in the refrigerator for up to 2 weeks.

SUPERFOOD SUPER-GOOD BLISS BALLS

Makes 30 balls
Prep time: 20 minutes

These are the perfect tasty snacks to pop into kids' lunchboxes or into your bag to nibble on while you are out (no getting tempted to buy junk food while you are on the run!). You can even add some protein powder to them and eat them as a little post-workout snack. They are delicious flavour bites that will definitely have you feeling great after eating them. They are a wonderful alternative to a chocolate truffle!

60 g (2 oz/½ cup) sunflower seeds
70 g (2½ oz/½ cup) pepitas (pumpkin seeds)
30 g (1 oz/¼ cup) chia seeds*
30 g (1 oz/½ cup) shredded coconut
40 g (1½ oz/¼ cup) brazil nuts
40 g (1½ oz/¼ cup) almonds
30 g (1 oz/¼ cup) hemp seeds*
2 tablespoons bee pollen* (optional)
1 tablespoon cinnamon
40 g (1½ oz) cacao powder*
1 scoop (35–40 g/1¼–1½ oz) of plant-based
   protein powder* (optional)
270 g (9½ oz) medjool dates*, pitted
60 ml (2 fl oz/¼ cup) coconut oil
1 teaspoon vanilla extract
80 ml (2½ fl oz/⅓ cup) rice malt syrup*
desiccated coconut for rolling

Place the sunflower seeds, pepitas, chia seeds and shredded coconut into a processor or blender and pulse until a fine meal is formed. Throw in the brazil nuts and almonds and pulse once or twice until they are crushed but not powdered (see note).

Transfer to a mixing bowl and add the hemp seeds, bee pollen, cinnamon, cacao and protein powder, if using.

In the now empty processor or blender, place the dates, coconut oil, vanilla and rice malt syrup and blend until smooth.

Place the liquid ingredients in the bowl with the dry ingredients and combine – you may need to get hands on and really mush the ingredients together if mixing with a spoon is not doing the trick (just make sure you wash your hands first!). Add a tablespoon of water if the mixture is too dry.

Next take about a tablespoon of mixture at a time and roll it into 2.5 cm (1 in) balls. Roll the balls in the desiccated coconut and place them in an airtight container in the freezer or refrigerator. These guys will keep for up to 2 weeks in the refrigerator, and a couple of months in the freezer.

Note: If you want a softer truffle, pulse the ingredients until everything is a fine meal.

SCONES

Makes 9 scones
Prep time: 15 minutes
Cooking time: 20 minutes

Scones, known as 'biscuits' in the US, have always been an absolute favourite of mine since I was young – from very early days when my nana used to them with jam and cream, to when I worked in a cafe during high school days watching my boss make the best scones in the world (in my opinion). My scones are a healthier take on the normally wheat-laden, buttery and dairy cream scones and are still just as light and beautiful to eat.

130 g (4½ oz/1 cup) buckwheat flour or
    150 g (5½ oz/1 cup) gluten-free plain
    (all-purpose) flour
40 g (1½ oz/¼ cup) superfine brown
    rice flour
25 g (1 oz/¼ cup) ground almonds
1 tablespoon flaxmeal*
2 teaspoons baking powder
2 tablespoons stevia* or xylitol*
¼ teaspoon salt
60 ml (2 fl oz/¼ cup) coconut cream
125 ml (4 fl oz/½ cup) plant-based milk*,
    plus extra for brushing
Berry chia jam (page 219) to serve
Whipped coconut cream (page 239) to serve

Combine the flours, ground almonds, flaxmeal, baking powder, stevia and salt in a bowl. Stir until everything is combined.

Make a well in the middle of the dry ingredients and add the coconut cream and milk. Using a knife, keep cutting it into the dough and gently stirring until everything is combined.

Preheat the oven to 180°C (350°F) and line a baking tray with baking paper.

Place the dough on a lightly floured surface and cut out your scones before transferring them to the prepared baking tray.

Brush the top of each scone with a little bit of extra milk and place in the oven. Bake for 20 minutes or until lightly golden on top.

Serve with berry chia jam and whipped coconut cream.

GINGER, ALMOND AND DATE COOKIES

These cookies are a staple in my household, and I always have a jar full of them. They are extremely easy to whip together and, while baking, they fill the house with a beautiful cookie smell!

Serves 16–20
Prep time: 15 minutes
Cooking time: 15 minutes

80 ml (2½ fl oz/⅓ cup) plant-based milk*
8 medjool dates*, pitted
1 tablespoon lucuma*
200 g (7 oz/2 cups) ground almonds
5 cm (2 in) piece fresh ginger, finely grated
1 teaspoon cinnamon
pinch of salt
2 tablespoons raw honey or rice malt syrup*
½ teaspoon mixed spice
¼ teaspoon ground ginger
30 g (1 oz/¼ cup) slivered almonds
35 g (1¼ oz/¼ cup) dark or dairy-free
  chocolate pieces or carob pieces
45 g (1½ oz/¼ cup) dates, pitted and
  quartered

Preheat the oven to 180°C (350°F) and line 1–2 baking trays with baking paper.

Place all the ingredients, except the almonds, chocolate and dates, in a food processor and blitz until relatively smooth and combined.

Transfer the mixture to a bowl and add the almonds, chocolate and dates. Stir with a spoon (or use your hands) until all the ingredients are evenly combined.

Take about a tablespoon of mixture, roll it into a ball and place on the prepared baking tray. Repeat with the remaining mixture, leaving about 2 cm (¾ in) between each ball. Flatten the balls down with the back of a spoon or fork and place into the oven. Bake for about 15 minutes or until golden.

Sneak a cookie while still warm (of course) and let the others cool down on the tray for about 10 minutes before transferring to a wire rack to cool completely.

Store in an airtight container for up to 1 week and enjoy! These family-friendly cookies won't last long!

TRIPLE CHOCOLATE COOKIES

These cookies are little pockets of deliciousness. I love to make them for any health food sceptic and any cookie lover. They are packed to the brim with antioxidants thanks to the cacao, and they are also grain- and nut-free, so suitable for many allergy sufferers!

Makes 18 cookies
Prep time: 15 minutes
Cooking time: 15 minutes

125 g (4½ oz/1 cup) sunflower seeds
60 g (2 oz/½ cup) black chia seeds*
2 tablespoons cacao powder*
30 g (1 oz/¼ cup) cacao nibs*
75 g (2¾ oz) chopped dark chocolate
  (at least 70% cocoa solids)
2 tablespoons maple syrup
60 ml (2 fl oz/¼ cup) flaxseed oil*
1 teaspoon vanilla extract
1 tablespoon lucuma*
¼ teaspoon baking powder
2 tablespoons coconut cream
pinch of salt

Place the sunflower and chia seeds in a blender or food processor and blitz until a powder is formed. Transfer to a bowl and mix in the rest of the ingredients.

Preheat the oven to 180°C (350°F) and line 1–2 baking trays with baking paper.

Form 18 even-sized balls, place them on the baking tray and press each ball down slightly. Bake for 15 minutes.

Remove from the oven, cool on the tray for 10 minutes, then eat! Store in an airtight container in the refrigerator for up to 1 week.

DINNER

*After a hard day's work, knowing you have
a healthy, delicious dinner ahead of you makes
everything seem easier, and it definitely helps
lift dampened spirits. Dinner is a time of
reflection and a time to reconnect with family
and friends and to share food with each other.*

*I remember being so grateful and in awe of my
mum when I was younger. She would get home
after a long day at work and still find time to
cook a beautiful meal for us. I didn't realise
then quite how talented and brilliant she was.
I would always compliment her on the food as
it blew my mind every time she cooked – how
did she make food taste THAT good? My mum
was never afraid to try something new. Today,
she is still an absolute kitchen superhero in my
eyes. She can turn the most random ingredients
in the refrigerator into something spectacular –
a skill that not many people have. She taught
me what I know today. She passed on her skills
and sat there and ate the food I made for her,
even if it was terrible!*

*I first started cooking dinner when I was in
high school as a way to make things easier
for my mum who already did a million and
one things for us. Many years on I still enjoy
cooking dinner and, more importantly, I love
sitting down to enjoy the meal, hearing stories,
telling jokes and soaking up the good vibes of
those around me.*

CAULIFLOWER 'RICE' DOLMA

Serves 4
Prep time: 10 minutes
Cooking time: 45 minutes

Dolma is something that was introduced to me by my Turkish boyfriend. One night he brought home dinner for me. It was the most beautiful-smelling thing, but I had no idea what it was. Capsicums (bell peppers), oily rice, amazing flavours – from that moment I was hooked! I knew I had to make my own version replacing the heavy rice with a much lighter cauliflower rice. Even my boyfriend gives this one his seal of approval and prefers to make it over the more traditional dolma!

½ head cauliflower
1 brown onion, diced
2 tablespoons plant-based oil*
200 g (7 oz/1 cup) tinned diced tomatoes
1 teaspoon sumac
1 teaspoon paprika
1 teaspoon allspice
1 teaspoon salt
1 teaspoon chilli flakes
75 g (2¾ oz/½ cup) currants
40 g (1½ oz/¼ cup) toasted pine nuts
15 g (½ oz/¼ cup) chopped dill
15 g (½ oz/¼ cup) chopped mint
7 g (¼ oz/¼ cup) chopped flat-leaf parsley
1 whole tomato, diced
60 ml (2 fl oz/¼ cup) olive oil
8 small or 4 large red capsicums
   (bell peppers)

Start by grating the cauliflower so it becomes a similar size to rice. Place it in a bowl and set aside.

In a saucepan or large frying pan over medium heat, cook the onion in the plant-based oil for 2–3 minutes until the onion is translucent. Add the cauliflower, tomato, sumac, paprika, allspice, salt and chilli flakes. Cook for 5–10 minutes until the cauliflower has soaked up the tomato liquid. Add the currants, toasted pine nuts and chopped herbs and cook for a further 2 minutes.

Stir the fresh diced tomato into the mixture along with the olive oil and cook for a further minute. Remove from the heat.

Preheat the oven to 180°C (350°F).

If using smaller capsicums, cut them in half and fill each half with the cauliflower mixture and place on a baking tray. If using large red capsicums, chop the tops off to use as 'lids'. Fill the capsicums with the cauliflower mixture and top with the lid and place into a small casserole dish so the capsicums are standing up touching each other. Cook for 20–30 minutes until the capsicums have softened and are ready to eat.

Serve and enjoy.

SWEET POTATO MUSHROOM BURGERS

Serves 4
Prep time: 15 minutes
Cooking time: 30 minutes

These burgers are definitely party stoppers. They will fool any meat-eater into thinking they are having a hearty burger, and yet there's no slab of meat or thick stodgy burger bun. Instead of being pregnant with a food baby after eating these and wanting to nap (like I do after I eat a regular burger) you will feel energised. The mushroom bun is a perfect replacement for bread and the taste combination is just incredible! I like to serve the burgers with a hot sauce and some Cashew 'goat's' cheese (page 220).

Mushroom burger

1 medium–large sweet potato
*400 g (14 oz) tinned chickpeas
   (garbanzo beans), drained and rinsed*
*2 tablespoons toasted sesame seeds,
   plus extra for rolling and sprinkling*
1 teaspoon ground cumin
¼ teaspoon cayenne pepper
½–1 teaspoon cinnamon
1 teaspoon turmeric
½ teaspoon chilli flakes
½ teaspoon salt
¼ teaspoon freshly ground black pepper
plant-based oil* for frying
8 large flat mushrooms
rocket (arugula) or baby English spinach
snow pea shoots to garnish

First steam the sweet potato for about 15 minutes or until soft. Once softened, place it in a mixing bowl with the chickpeas. Now get mashing. You still want the mixture to be quite chunky, so don't make it super-smooth. Add the sesame seeds, spices (see note), chilli flakes, salt and pepper and mix it all up. Don't be put off by the fact that the mixture is still like mashed potato (as essentially it is).

Grab a handful of the mixture and pat it into a ball. Roll it gently in sesame seeds and set aside. The mixture will make around 8 patties, so you can either make yourselves 2 burgers each (just double the mushrooms needed) or just serve an extra patty on the side of your burger.

>   >

Edamame guacamole

175 g (6 oz/1 cup) edamame* (soy beans),
    podded
1 avocado
3 garlic cloves
15 g (½ oz/¼ cup) chopped coriander
    (cilantro) leaves
juice of 1 lime
1 tablespoon olive or coconut oil
¼ teaspoon cayenne pepper
salt

Caramelised onion

1 red onion, halved and cut into slices
1 tablespoon maple syrup
1 tablespoon plant-based oil*

For the edamame guacamole, first steam the edamame for about 2 minutes. Transfer to a food processor or blender with the remaining ingredients and blitz to the desired texture. Set aside.

To make the caramelised onion, cook the onion in a small saucepan or frying pan with the maple syrup and plant-based oil over medium heat until translucent and cooked, about 5 minutes. Set aside.

Now to fry the burgers! Heat some oil in a frying pan over medium heat and add the patties to the pan. You have to be careful when flipping these babies – don't be alarmed if they squish a bit! Cook the patties for 3–4 minutes on each side.

While cooking your patties, in another frying pan over medium heat, sauté your mushrooms in a little oil until cooked, about 5 minutes. If you don't have 2 frying pans, cook the patties first and place them in a 150–180°C (300–350°F) oven to keep warm. Or you can just cook your mushrooms in the oven at 180°C (350°F) with a drizzle of oil for 20 minutes – or even have them raw!

Next assemble your burgers. Place 1 mushroom on the plate, put a patty on top and then some guacamole, caramelised onion, rocket and snow pea shoots. Place a second mushroom on top. Sprinkle the top mushroom with sesame seeds. Enjoy!

Note: You can play around with the spices. Your tastebuds may like more or less of one spice or another, so it's all about tasting as you go!

ARTICHOKE PAELLA

Serves 4
Prep time: 5 minutes
Cooking time: 30 minutes

Paella brings back memories of family and friends sitting around the table, and mum bringing out a HUGE paella dish about a third of the size of the table, with everyone digging in, talking and laughing. Paella is one of those dishes that makes an impact on the table and brings everyone together. It's simple, flavoursome and you will feel like you're in the heart of Spain with each and every mouthful.

½ teaspoon saffron threads
1 teaspoon salt
1 litre (34 fl oz/4 cups) low-sodium faux
   chicken or fish stock
2 tablespoons plant-based oil*
1 brown onion, diced
2 garlic cloves, crushed
1 large tomato, diced
1 red capsicum (bell pepper), diced
200 g (7 oz/1 cup) long-grain brown rice
1 teaspoon smoked paprika
400 g (14 oz) tinned artichoke hearts,
   drained and rinsed, whole or cut into
   wedges
80 g (2¾ oz/½ cup) frozen peas
15 g (½ oz/½ cup) chopped flat-leaf parsley
   to serve
lemon wedges to serve

Grind the saffron and salt in a mortar and pestle. Mix the mixture with the stock in a bowl and set aside.

Heat the oil in a large paella pan, or individual smaller paella dishes, over medium heat and add the onion and garlic. Cook for 2–3 minutes or until the onion begins to turn translucent. Add the tomato and capsicum and cook for a further 2 minutes. Add the rice and paprika, stir and cook for another 2 minutes. Add the saffron-infused stock, stir then allow to come to the boil. Cook for 15 minutes then add the artichoke hearts. Sprinkle over the peas and continue to cook for another 2–3 minutes.

Remove the pan from the heat, sprinkle over the chopped parsley and serve with the lemon wedges.

HOMEMADE PIZZAS

Serves 4
Prep time: 20 minutes,
  plus 45 minutes rising
Cooking time: 40 minutes

Pizzas are a must in a person's life – not greasy fat-laden pizzas, though! This recipe is for delicious and simple vegan pizzas. You can top them with more or less ingredients depending on what you fancy. The dough is easy to make and the whole thing is so flavoursome. This dish is sure to please the family!

Pizza dough
260 g (9 oz/2 cups) buckwheat flour
200 g (7 oz/1¼ cups) brown rice flour
7 g (¼ oz) dry yeast
1 teaspoon salt
2 tablespoons coconut sugar*
2 tablespoons plant-based oil*

 Tomato sauce for base
375 g (13 oz/2½ cups) cherry tomatoes
3 garlic cloves
2 tablespoons plant-based oil*
½ teaspoon salt
¼ teaspoon freshly ground black pepper

To make the pizza dough, begin by combining the flours, yeast, salt and sugar in an electric mixer with the bread hook attachment. Add 250 ml (8½ fl oz/1 cup) water and the plant-based oil and mix until a nice smooth dough has formed.

Transfer the dough to a lightly floured work surface and gently knead for 5–10 minutes. Place in an oiled bowl in a warm place for 35–45 minutes or until risen.

Preheat the oven to 180°C (350°F).

While the dough is proving, make the tomato sauce. In a small oven dish place the tomatoes, garlic, oil and salt and pepper. Bake for 15–20 minutes until nice and roasted (see note). Remove and transfer the mixture to a food processor or blender and blitz into a sauce.

>   >

Topping

75 g (2¾ oz/½ cup) cherry tomatoes, halved
1 zucchini (courgette), thinly sliced
¼ teaspoon salt
¼ teaspoon freshly ground black pepper
¼ teaspoon kelp
1 red onion, chopped
1 teaspoon plant-based oil*
2 tablespoons maple syrup
1 bunch basil leaves

You can also add:

sliced mushrooms
capsicum (bell pepper) slices
artichoke hearts
Cashew 'goat's' cheese (page 220)

Knead the dough again, before pushing it into 2 flat bases on 2 baking or pizza trays. You can make the bases any shape you like – round, square or rectangular, it's up to you! You do want to get the bases quite thin (about 5 mm/¼ in) and, then, once in the desired shape, prick them with a fork to stop them from rising too much in the cooking process.

Bake the bases in the oven for 5–10 minutes then remove.

Spread the sauce onto the bases and top with the tomatoes, zucchini, salt, pepper and kelp. In a small frying pan, fry the onion in the oil and maple syrup for 5–10 minutes. Add this to the top of the pizza.

Cook for 15–20 minutes until the base and vegetables are nice and cooked. Remove from the oven, slice, top with fresh basil and enjoy!

Note: When I have a lot of time, I prefer to slow-roast the vegetables for the sauce over a couple of hours. But when we are making a speedy pizza, the quick roast works fine!

CHIPOTLE BLACK BEAN TACOS

Serves 4–5
Prep time: 30 minutes, plus resting
Cooking time: 30 minutes

Mexican is my all-time favourite cuisine, and I particularly love Mexican street food. I created this taco recipe as I wanted something that was as easy and quick to make as a supermarket taco kit, but the authentic taste of a true Mexican feast. I have never had a bad review of this recipe and would happily challenge any famous Mexican restaurant with it!

<u>Tortillas</u>
125 g (4½ oz/1¼ cups) masa harina* or stoneground maize flour (see note)
½ teaspoon salt
150–200 ml (5–7 fl oz) lukewarm water
coconut oil for frying

<u>Chipotle black beans</u>
2 smoked chipotle chillies*, dried or tinned (if dried, soak in hot water until softened)
1 red chilli
1 small red capsicum (bell pepper)
400 g (14 oz) tinned diced tomatoes
1 teaspoon cumin seeds
½ teaspoon sweet paprika
½ red onion
400 g (14 oz) tinned black beans, drained and rinsed

<u>Grilled corn salsa</u>
1 tablespoon coconut oil
200 g (7 oz) fresh or frozen (defrosted) corn kernels
½ green capsicum (bell pepper), diced
½ red onion, finely chopped
¼ bunch coriander (cilantro) leaves, chopped
juice of ½ lime

For the tortillas, put the flour and salt in a mixing bowl and gradually add the lukewarm water as you work the ingredients together with your hands to form a dough. Cover with plastic wrap and let the dough rest for 15 minutes.

Get the dough in your hands and break it up into 8–10 equal parts and form small balls of dough. If you have a tortilla press, place each ball in the press and press to create the tortilla (see note). Otherwise, simply roll out each tortilla into a large flat circular shape, about 2 mm (⅛ in) thick, using a rolling pin.

Put a small amount of coconut oil in a non-stick frying pan and cook your tortillas, one at a time, on medium heat. If you see them puff up this is good. Once one side is becoming golden, after about 2–3 minutes, flip and cook the other side for another 2–3 minutes.

Try to use the cooked tortillas within 2 hours of making, though the dough can be made in advance a few days before then wrapped in plastic wrap and stored in the refrigerator. If you are making the dough in advance, keep it in the refrigerator but make sure you remove it 20–30 minutes before using it.

>   >

Red cabbage slaw
¼ red cabbage, sliced
¼ bunch coriander (cilantro) leaves,
   chopped
60 g (2 oz/¼ cup) vegan mayonnaise
juice of ½ lime

To serve
Edamame guacamole (page 108)
Cashew 'goat's' cheese (page 220)
seeds from ½ pomegranate
2 limes, cut into wedges
cayenne pepper
50 g (1¾ oz/1 cup) coriander (cilantro)
   leaves, chopped
Simple hot sauce (page 232) or Tabasco

For the chipotle black beans, place the chipotle chillies, red chilli, capsicum, tomato, cumin seeds, paprika and red onion in a food processor and blitz until you have a smooth salsa. Transfer to a saucepan. Add the black beans and cook on medium heat for 10 minutes. Set aside and keep warm.

For the grilled corn salsa, heat the coconut oil in the frying pan, add the corn and capsicum and fry until golden over medium heat for about 10 minutes – you need to leave these vegetables on for longer than you think to give them a good golden glow; don't be tempted to pull them off the stove early! Place the vegetables in a bowl with the onion, coriander and lime juice. Set aside and keep warm.

For the slaw, place the cabbage in a mixing bowl with the coriander, mayonnaise and lime juice. Mix together and place in the refrigerator until you're ready to go.

Once all your components are made, give each person 2 tortillas. Top with chipotle black beans, slaw, grilled corn salsa, guacamole and, to amp it up even more, sprinkle with a little cashew 'goat's' cheese and pomegranate seeds. Serve with lime wedges, a sprinkling of cayenne pepper, the coriander and the hot sauce! Yum!

Notes: Any masa harina or any stoneground maize flour is fine. Just note that the flour should not have any other ingredients except maize in it and it should be GMO-free.

If you don't have a tortilla press, I do suggest investing in one as they are quite affordable and are amazing for making homemade wraps and tortillas.

COTTAGE PIES WITH ROOT VEGETABLE MASH

Serves 5–6
Prep time: 15 minutes
Cooking time: 50 minutes

This dish is an absolute winter favourite of mine. It's comforting, it's warming and it's a dish that brings the whole family together on freezing cold nights – and a smile to many cold miserable faces. It's my take on the classic cottage pie, which is normally made with meat and white potato mash. Though my memories of the classic cottage pie are of it being delicious, I knew there was a way to make it vegan and healthier. This version is packed with vitamins, and meat and white potatoes are nowhere to be seen! It makes the perfect dinner at the end of a long hard day at work, or even post-workout. It will make your insides warm and happy. You can serve the individual pies on their own or with a green salad.

Filling
1 onion, diced
2 garlic cloves, crushed
1 tablespoon plant-based oil*
1 carrot, finely chopped
2 celery stalks, diced
salt and freshly ground black pepper to taste
400 g (14 oz) tinned diced tomatoes
1 bay leaf
1 rosemary sprig
1 thyme sprig, plus extra leaves to garnish
½ teaspoon dried marjoram
400 g (14 oz) tinned brown lentils, drained and rinsed, or faux minced (ground) meat
2 teaspoons Simple hot sauce (page 232) or Tabasco
1 teaspoon balsamic vinegar or to taste   >

For the filling, sauté the onion and garlic in the plant-based oil in a medium saucepan over medium heat until translucent. Add the carrot and celery and season with salt and pepper to taste. Cook the mixture until the vegetables are tender, about 10 minutes. Add the tinned tomatoes, herbs and brown lentils or faux mince. Leave to simmer for 10 minutes until the lentils are tender or the faux mince is warmed through. Add the hot sauce and balsamic vinegar and stir them through. Check the seasoning again.

>

Root vegetable mash

1 sweet potato, skin left on
1 parsnip
¼ head cauliflower
1 small leek, diced
1 garlic clove, crushed
small handful of sage leaves
1 tablespoon plant-based oil*
salt and freshly ground black pepper
splash of soy milk or coconut cream
1 teaspoon maple syrup

For the mash, steam the sweet potato and then the parsnip and cauliflower separately, for 15–20 minutes until tender.

In a small frying pan, sauté the leek and garlic with a couple of snipped sage leaves for 2 minutes in the plant-based oil. Season with salt and pepper and allow to cook on low heat for a further 5 minutes. Once the leek is translucent, transfer the leek and sage mixture to a blender with the steamed cauliflower and parsnips. Add a splash of milk and pulse until just mashed.

Preheat the oven to 180°C (350°F).

In a separate bowl, roughly mash the sweet potato by hand. Add it to the blender mixture and mix to combine. Season with salt and pepper and add an extra dash of milk if too dry. Add the maple syrup and set aside.

Place the lentil mixture into 5–6 small ramekins or one big dish. Top with the mash mixture and put the extra thyme on the top of each pie.

Bake in the oven for 30 minutes until crisp on top with bubbling sides and then serve.

GINGER PHO SOUP

Serves 4
Prep time: 10 minutes
Cooking time: 30 minutes

I love pho. However, after each time I had a bowl of pho in a Vietnamese restaurant I would feel lethargic. This recipe is a very simple yet flavoursome vegan version that I came up with to satisfy my cravings, yet allow my body to feel super-nourished and energetic after eating.

200 g (7 oz/2 cups) shiitake mushrooms, sliced
200 g (7 oz) firm tofu
1 tablespoon plant-based oil*
245 g (8½ oz) brown rice noodles*

Broth
1 litre (34 fl oz/4 cups) low-sodium vegetable stock
6 star anise
1 cinnamon stick
2 teaspoons ground ginger
6 cloves
2 black cardamom pods
2 spring onions (scallions), chopped
1 teaspoon dried brown onion
2 cm (¾ in) piece fresh ginger
juice of 1 lime
3 teaspoons tamari

To serve
4 spring onions (scallions), chopped
90 g (3 oz/1 cup) bean sprouts
1 bunch bok choy (pak choy), chopped
50 g (1¾ oz/1 cup) Thai basil leaves
30 g (1 oz/1 cup) coriander (cilantro) leaves
2 limes
1 tablespoon tamari

To make the broth, put the stock, spices, spring onions, dried onion, fresh ginger, lime juice, 500 ml (17 fl oz/2 cups) water and the tamari in a saucepan over medium heat. Simmer for 20 minutes, adding more water as required.

Meanwhile, in a small frying pan over medium heat, cook the shiitake mushrooms and tofu in the plant-based oil for 5–10 minutes. Set aside.

About 5 minutes before serving, strain the broth and return the liquid back to the saucepan. Add the noodles to the broth. Cook the noodles for 5–10 minutes and remove from the heat just before they become tender.

Divide the noodles between 4 bowls and pour over the broth. Top with the spring onions, bean sprouts, bok choy, tofu and mushroom mixture, Thai basil and coriander. Serve with half a lime and extra tamari to season.

TOP TO BOTTOM:
GARLIC NAAN,
RAJMA, COCONUT
VEGETABLE CURRY

INDIAN FEAST: RAJMA, COCONUT VEGETABLE CURRY AND GARLIC NAAN

Serves 5–6
Prep time: 30 minutes, plus rising
Cooking time: 1 hour

Last year I was lucky enough to go to South America. Though this recipe is not South American, it evolved from that trip. One night while sitting in the apartment deciding where to go for dinner, we got a knock on the door. An Indian man, with whom my dad was working, brought us an array of curries his wife had made. The first thing that captivated me was the amazing smell – it filled the apartment instantly. Next was the taste. Oh boy, I can't even express how wonderful those curries tasted. Every single tastebud came alive. There was a brilliant balance of flavours and tastes I had never experienced before. Being the food-obsessed person I am, I could not leave without getting the recipes, and the lady was kind enough to pass on her secret recipes. So I present to you part of that Indian feast: a delicious rajma, my favourite curry from that night and also a recipe for vegan naan bread which, hands down, is one of my ultimate gluten-free staples. My mind still explodes at the simplicity and insane flavours of these dishes. Trust me, they will blow your regular Indian takeaway out of the park!

Rajma
2 tablespoons plant-based* or coconut oil
2 teaspoons black cumin seeds
3–5 cloves
1 teaspoon cinnamon
1 tablespoon garlic and ginger paste*
1 onion, thinly sliced
1 green chilli
1 teaspoon chilli powder
½ teaspoon turmeric
salt
1 teaspoon chana masala*
400 g (14 oz) tinned diced tomatoes
400 g (14 oz) tinned red kidney beans or
  a combination of 200 g (7 oz) tinned
  chickpeas (garbanzo beans) and
  200 g (7 oz) tinned black beans, drained
  and rinsed

The first thing to cook is the rajma. Heat the oil in a medium saucepan over medium heat and fry the black cumin seeds, cloves, cinnamon and the garlic and ginger paste for 1–2 minutes or until fragrant. Once the seeds begin to crack, add the onion, green chilli, chilli powder, turmeric, salt and chana masala. Cook for 2 minutes or until the onion starts to become translucent.

Add the tomatoes, kidney beans and 125 ml (4 fl oz/½ cup) water and cook for 10 minutes. Test a bean to see if it's done. Do not shake or stir the rajma mix. Cook for a further 5 minutes on low. Set aside.

>

>

Garlic naan
1 tablespoon rice malt syrup*
2 teaspoons dry yeast
125 ml (4 fl oz/½ cup) rice or almond milk
1 tablespoon apple cider vinegar
130 g (4½ oz/¾ cup) white rice flour
125 g (4½ oz/¾ cup) brown rice flour
30 g (1 oz/¼ cup) cornflour (cornstarch)
30 g (1 oz/¼ cup) potato starch*
2 teaspoons guar gum*
1½ teaspoons sea salt
¼ teaspoon baking powder
60 ml (2 fl oz/¼ cup) coconut oil
2 flax eggs* ('no egg' replacement mix)

Coconut vegetable curry
115 g (4 oz/1 cup) coconut powder
2 teaspoons poppy seeds
2 tablespoons coconut oil
1 onion, thinly sliced
1 teaspoon garlic and ginger paste*
¼ teaspoon turmeric
pinch of salt
¼ teaspoon chilli powder
60 g (2 oz/½ cup) green beans, chopped
1 carrot, diced
1 potato or sweet potato, diced
1 head cauliflower, in small florets
50 g (1¾ oz/1 cup) English spinach, chopped
555 g (1 lb 4 oz/3 cups) firm tofu, cubed
60 g (2 oz/½ cup) sultanas (golden raisins)

To serve
mixed dried fruits
1 tablespoon coconut oil
chopped coriander (cilantro) leaves
green chillies, sliced
cooked brown rice
60 ml (2 fl oz/¼ cup) coconut cream

For the garlic naan, mix 125 ml (4 fl oz/½ cup) water, the rice malt syrup and yeast and whisk until frothy. Set aside for 10–15 minutes. If the mixture does not froth up, discard it and start again.

In a pitcher, mix the milk and apple cider vinegar together and set aside for 15 minutes to curdle.

In a mixing bowl, combine the flours, potato starch, guar gum, salt and baking powder and mix together with a wooden spoon. Next add all the liquids and combine. The mixture should end up looking a bit like mashed potato. Cover the bowl with plastic wrap and place it in a warm place for around 20 minutes to rise.

For the coconut vegetable curry, put the coconut powder and poppy seeds in a large saucepan and toss in the pan over medium heat until warm and light brown. Add 375 ml (12½ fl oz/1½ cups) water and stir to make a paste. Then add the oil, onion, garlic and ginger paste, turmeric, salt and chilli powder and sauté for 5 minutes. Once the onion is translucent add all the chopped vegetables and the tofu. Simmer until the vegetables are tender and then add the sultanas. Keep warm over very low heat.

Get the risen naan dough and divide it into 6 balls. Shape the balls into flat naan bread shapes (around 1 cm/½ in thick). Cook 1 or 2 at a time in a non-stick pan over medium heat. You can grease the pan with coconut oil if required.

Fry the mixed dried fruit in the oil in a frying pan over medium heat for 5 minutes or until crisp. Serve the rajma and coconut curry with chopped coriander and green chillies sprinkled on top. Top the coconut curry with the chopped dried fruits and serve everything with some brown rice, coconut cream and the just-fried naan.

MACROBIOTIC BALANCING BOWL

Serves 1
Prep time: 10 minutes
Cooking time: 15 minutes

I was first introduced to the macrobiotic diet by my friend Diem. I had heard of it, but I had never actually researched it. The macrobiotic diet is about balance. Diem turned towards it for its healing properties. I have since become very attached to this particular approach to food, and it's something I try to incorporate into my everyday life. So here for you is my little take on a simple macrobiotic bowl to keep your yin and yang in balance.

55 g (2 oz/¼ cup) short-grain or other brown rice
½ teaspoon tamari
½ teaspoon miso paste*
1 teaspoon black sesame seeds
½ carrot
75 g (2¾ oz/⅓ cup) tinned or dried chickpeas (garbanzo beans), drained and rinsed if tinned, soaked for 12 hours in water if dried
45 g (1½ oz/⅓ cup) sauerkraut or fermented vegetables
35 g (1¼ oz/½ cup) kale, chopped
80 g (2¾ oz/½ cup) bok choy (pak choy), chopped
¼ teaspoon kelp powder
¼ avocado, stoned
1 teaspoon shredded nori*

Bring 250 ml (8½ fl oz/1 cup) water to the boil in a saucepan over medium heat and add the brown rice. Reduce the heat to low and cook the rice for 10–15 minutes until tender. Strain the rice and transfer to a bowl. Mix in the tamari, miso paste and sesame seeds and place the rice in the centre of your serving bowl. (You will place all the other ingredients in separate piles in a circle around the rice.)

Using a vegetable peeler, peel strands of the carrot and neatly place to one side of the rice in the bowl.

Place the chickpeas and sauerkraut in separate piles around the rice.

Rub the kale gently to soften it and then also place it in the bowl.

Gently steam the bok choy with the kelp powder sprinkled on top for 1 minute and then place it in the bowl.

Cut the avocado into small pieces and also place it in the bowl.

Top the rice with the nori and serve. Chew slowly and mindfully and enjoy.

JAPANESE MISO EGGPLANT WITH TAMARI SOBA

Japanese cooking is up there in my list of favourite cuisines. It is so inspiring and fresh. Making Japanese food is as simple as buying it from the local sushi shop, and this is by far my favourite dish to make at home. The flavours will fill your mouth with joy and it's also wholesome and nourishing.

Serves 2
Prep time: 5 minutes
Cooking time: 30 minutes

1 large eggplant (aubergine)
45 g (1½ oz) miso paste*
1 tablespoon plant-based oil*
100 g (3½ oz) buckwheat soba noodles
65 g (2¼ oz) enoki mushrooms*
2 tablespoons sesame oil
2 tablespoons organic tamari
50 g (1¾ oz/⅓ cup) frozen edamame (soy beans)*

To serve
fresh wasabi
pickled ginger
tamari
sesame seeds to sprinkle

Preheat the oven to 180°C (350°F) and line a baking tray with baking paper.

Cut the eggplant into 5–6 wedges lengthways. Rub the wedges with 2 tablespoons of the miso paste and the plant-based oil, then place on the baking tray.

Cook the eggplant for 20–30 minutes until golden and soft, turning the eggplant wedges over half-way through cooking.

In a saucepan of boiling water, cook the soba noodles for 5–10 minutes until just al dente. Strain, rinse and set aside in a bowl of cold water to prevent the noodles from cooking further and sticking together.

Cut the ends off the enoki mushrooms and wash them thoroughly. Place them in a frying pan over medium heat with the sesame oil and cook for 2 minutes. Add the remaining miso paste and tamari and cook for 1 minute. Add the edamame and the soba noodles, coating them in the tamari and miso sauce. Turn off the heat. The edamame should still have a slight crunch and be vibrant in colour.

Place the noodles and greens on a plate then top with the roasted miso eggplant. Serve with wasabi, pickled ginger and extra tamari and sprinkle over the sesame seeds.

GREEN PUMPKIN CURRY WITH CRISPY BLACK RICE CAKES

This is another beautiful recipe contributed by Diem Ly Vo and it will absolutely blow your tastebuds away. It's simple to make and the flavours are like nothing you have tasted before. It leaves your body singing after eating. It looks like a work of art and will make you want to throw your local takeaway curry in the bin! It's great served with a bowl of crisp greens like lettuce and rocket (arugula).

Serves 4 or 2 very hungry people
Prep time: 20 minutes, plus cooling
Cooking time: 40 minutes

Black rice cakes
200 g (7 oz/1 cup) black rice*
1 teaspoon sea salt
1 tablespoon plant-based oil*

For the rice cakes, bring the rice, 500 ml (17 fl oz/2 cups) water and the sea salt to the boil over medium heat. Then reduce the heat to low and let the rice simmer until it is cooked through and all the water has evaporated, about 30 minutes.

Let the rice cool and then refrigerate (overnight is best).

Lightly oil your hands to prevent the rice from sticking and form the rice into 4 square 7.5 cm (3 in) patties. Compress the rice as much as possible to prevent it from breaking apart when frying.

Heat the plant-based oil in a cast-iron pan over high heat and, before the oil starts to smoke, fry the rice patties for about 2 minutes on each side or until the outside becomes crispy.

>   >

Mushrooms
100 g (3½ oz) oyster mushrooms
1 tablespoon plant-based oil*
½ teaspoon sea salt
½ teaspoon freshly ground black pepper

Green pumpkin curry
300 g (10½ oz/2 cups) chopped pumpkin
   (winter squash)
250 ml (8½ fl oz/1 cup) low-sodium
   vegetable stock
2 tablespoons green curry paste
2 kaffir lime leaves
75 g (2¾ oz/½ cup) sliced bamboo shoots
60 ml (2 fl oz/¼ cup) full-fat coconut milk
mint leaves to serve

For the mushrooms, toss them in the oil, salt and pepper. Sear them in the same pan as the rice, either at the same time if your pan is big enough, or after.

For the curry, bring the pumpkin and 500 ml (17 fl oz/2 cups) water to a boil over high heat, then reduce the heat to medium–low and simmer until the pumpkin is very tender and almost all the water has evaporated, about 30 minutes. However, be careful not to burn the pumpkin!

Add the vegetable stock, curry paste, kaffir lime leaves and bamboo shoots and simmer for 7–10 minutes. (While the curry is simmering, I use a spoon to smash most of the pumpkin because I prefer a smoother, thicker curry, but you don't have to.)

Add the coconut milk and simmer for another minute or so before turning off the heat.

Divide the curry between serving bowls. Top with the rice cakes, mushrooms and a couple of mint leaves. (Place the rice cakes on just before serving as they can quickly soak up the curry and become soggy if put on too early.) Serve immediately.

RAINBOW THAI STIR-FRY

Serves 4
Prep time: 10 minutes
Cooking time: 10 minutes

If I am ever tired and don't know what to make when I come home from work, this is usually what I end up cooking. It's mind-numbingly easy. It's also so colourful that it will turn any miserable day into a happy one, and there will be no need to call the local Thai takeaway ever again. I cannot over-emphasise the vibrant flavours in this dish — think pad thai, but so, so, so much better!

Sauce

1 tablespoon tamarind paste
2 tablespoons coconut sugar*
1 kaffir lime leaf
1 lemongrass stem
2 garlic cloves
5 cm (2 in) piece fresh ginger
1 tablespoon tamari
juice of 1 lime
2 tablespoons sesame oil
2 tablespoons almond oil

Stir-fry

½ red onion, diced
1 carrot, julienned
⅛ purple cabbage, thinly sliced
2 red chillies, sliced
100 g (3½ oz) whole oyster mushrooms
   or sliced shiitake mushrooms
50 g (1¾ oz) enoki mushrooms*
1 teaspoon kelp
125 g (4½ oz) flat brown rice noodles*
1 bunch broccolini, stalks cut into thirds

Garnish

½ bunch coriander (cilantro) leaves,
   chopped
2 limes, quartered
40 g (1½ oz/¼ cup) peanuts, crushed
2 spring onions (scallions), chopped

Place all the sauce ingredients in a food processor or blender and blitz until smooth. Set aside.

Heat a wok or large frying pan over medium heat and add the sauce and onion. Cook for 2–3 minutes then add the carrot, cabbage, chillies, mushrooms and kelp and cook for 5 minutes.

Meanwhile cook the noodles for 5 minutes in a pan of boiling water. Remove from the heat, drain and run under cool water.

Add the broccolini to the wok along with the noodles and cook for a further 2 minutes.

Serve in bowls and top with coriander, lime wedges, the peanuts and spring onions.

SPAGHETTI AND 'MEATBALLS'

Serves 4–5
Prep time: 15 minutes
Cooking time: 30 minutes

Spaghetti and meatballs has always been a favourite in my house. However, after I stopped eating meat about 12 years ago it kind of drifted off the rotating menu. I tried various things like lentil bolognese and faux meat sauces, which were all delicious, but I still missed the humble meatball. When I created this recipe I was beyond chuffed! The meatballs are full of flavour and go perfectly with the simple tomato sauce. This is enough to convert any meat-eater into being vegan for the night.

400 g (14 oz) gluten-free spaghetti
basil to garnish

Meatballs
1 brown onion, diced
1 tablespoon plant-based oil*
400 g (14 oz) tinned brown lentils, drained
    and rinsed
180 g (6½ oz/2 cups) sliced button
    mushrooms
1 bay leaf
½ teaspoon dried marjoram
½ bunch flat-leaf parsley
2 garlic cloves, crushed
50 g (1¾ oz/½ cup) gluten-free oats
    or flaked quinoa*
2 tablespoons flaxmeal*
1 tablespoon tomato paste (concentrated
    purée)
1 low-sodium faux beef stock cube

Tomato sauce
1 onion, diced
1 tablespoon plant-based oil*
2 teaspoons crushed garlic
1 teaspoon dried oregano
½ teaspoon dried marjoram
pinch of pink lake salt*
1 teaspoon stevia*
1 teaspoon finely chopped chilli
700 ml (23½ fl oz) passata (puréed
    tomatoes)

For the meatballs, blitz the onion in a food processor until very finely diced. Transfer to a large frying pan over medium heat with the plant-based oil.

Now blitz the lentils and mushrooms in the food processor for 10–20 seconds or until chopped but not mush. Add the herbs, garlic, oats, flaxmeal and 125 ml (4 fl oz/½ cup) water. Blitz again for 10–20 seconds or until it is beginning to come together. Transfer the mixture to the frying pan with the onions and add the tomato paste and stock cube. Cook for 5–10 minutes then remove from the heat. Allow to cool slightly before handling.

Preheat the oven to 180°C (350°F) and line a baking tray with baking paper.

Roll the mixture into 4 cm (1½ in) balls and place them on the baking tray. Bake for 15–20 minutes or until they are just crunchy on the outside.

For the sauce, cook the onion in the oil in a pan over medium heat until translucent. Add the remaining ingredients, reduce the heat to low and simmer for 20 minutes.

Cook the spaghetti in boiling salted water for 8–10 minutes or until al dente. Drain and place in serving bowls. Top with the meatballs and a big spoonful of tomato sauce. Add some micro basil and serve.

SPRING GREEN LASAGNE

This recipe is a twist on normal lasagne and is packed with beautiful green vegetables. There is no meat in sight, nor cheese, nor gluten. It is as healthy as it is delicious, and is a great way to trick even the fussiest kids (or adults) into eating green vegetables!

Serves 4
Prep time: 10 minutes
Cooking time: 45 minutes

4 French shallots, diced
2 tablespoons plant-based oil*
3 garlic cloves, crushed
1 teaspoon salt
1 tablespoon capers
1 quantity Cashew 'goat's' cheese (page 220)
250 ml (8½ fl oz/1 cup) coconut cream
250 ml (8½ fl oz/1 cup) low-sodium
   vegetable stock
zest of 1 lemon
juice of ½ lemon
25 g (1 oz/½ cup) chopped mint
15 g (½ oz/¼ cup) chopped basil
7 g (¼ oz/¼ cup) chopped flat-leaf parsley
80 g (2¾ oz/½ cup) peas
95 g (3¼ oz/½ cup) broad (fava) beans
1 bunch asparagus, chopped
1 bunch broccolini, chopped
2 kale leaves, chopped
250 g (9 oz) gluten-free lasagne sheets

Cook the shallots in the plant-based oil in a large saucepan over medium heat for 5 minutes. Add the garlic, salt and capers and cook for another 2 minutes. Add the 'goat's' cheese, coconut cream, vegetable stock and lemon zest and juice. Once the mixture begins to thicken, after about 5 minutes, add the mint, basil and parsley. Remove from the heat and keep warm.

While the sauce is thickening, steam the peas, broad beans, asparagus and broccolini for 5 minutes. In the last minute add the chopped kale and immediately remove from the heat.

Preheat the oven to 180°C (350°F).

In a lasagne dish, begin by spreading a small spoonful of sauce over the bottom of the dish, top with lasagne sheets then add a good serving of the steamed vegetables. Top with more sauce and another layer of lasagne sheets. Repeat this 2–3 times or until out of mixture. Spoon sauce onto the top lasagne sheet and bake in the oven for 20–30 minutes or until the mixture is bubbling and the top is crisp.

Serve with a salad or on its own!

SPINACH GNOCCHI WITH BASIL PESTO

Gnocchi has to be one of the best types of pasta. It is surprisingly easy (and quick) to make and will fill you up. This is a gluten- and grain-free version, perfect for those with an intolerance. When paired with the pesto it will blow your socks off!

Serves 5
Prep time: 10 minutes, plus drying
Cooking time: 30 minutes

Spinach gnocchi
2 kg (4 lb 6 oz) potatoes, peeled and chopped
300 g (10½ oz) English spinach, chopped
1 teaspoon salt
260 g (9 oz/2 cups) buckwheat flour
basil leaves to serve

Basil pesto
100 g (3½ oz/2 cups) basil
almond oil
olive oil
2 garlic cloves
zest of 1 lemon
40 g (1½ oz/¼ cup) pine nuts
2 tablespoons cashews
40 g (1½ oz/¼ cup) almonds

To make the gnocchi, start by steaming the potatoes until soft, around 15 minutes. Transfer them to a bowl with the spinach and mash until smooth. Add the salt and flour and, using your hands, gently work the mixture to make a dough.

Sprinkle a work surface with flour and roll the dough into 2.5 × 1 cm (1 × ½ in) cylinders and chop into 2.5 cm (1 in) pieces. Gently flatten the top of each gnocchi with a fork and set aside to dry for about 20 minutes.

For the pesto, combine all the ingredients in a food processor or blender and blitz until smooth but still chunky (or to your desired pesto consistency).

To cook the gnocchi, place them in boiling hot water and when they rise to the top, remove them.

Toss the gnocchi in the pesto and serve with micro basil leaves on top.

WILD MUSHROOM RISOTTO

Serves 4
Prep time: 5 minutes
Cooking time: 25 minutes

This is my recipe of choice when I know I have someone coming over but am too tired to cook. It is so simple and lets the rice cooker do most of the work, so you can put your feet up or entertain without worrying about the dinner! It's amazingly tasty and one of my favourite comforting meals.

60 ml (2 fl oz/¼ cup) plant-based oil*
1 brown onion, diced
440 g (15½ oz/2 cups) brown rice
1 litre (34 fl oz/4 cups) low-sodium faux
    chicken stock
1 teaspoon dried marjoram
1 teaspoon dried thyme
1¼ teaspoons salt
250 ml (8½ fl oz/1 cup) white wine
200 g (7 oz/2 cups) mushrooms (such
    as enoki*, shiitake, porcini or button
    mushrooms), finely sliced
½ teaspoon ground kelp
¼ teaspoon freshly ground black pepper
15 g (½ oz/½ cup) chopped flat-leaf parsley
    for garnish

Put 1 tablespoon of the plant-based oil and the onion in a rice cooker or large saucepan. Once the onion begins to turn translucent, add the rice and fry for another minute.

Add the stock, herbs and salt and cook for 10 minutes. Stir and add the white wine. Cook for another 5–10 minutes, stirring occasionally, until cooked. Let the risotto stay warm in the rice cooker.

Meanwhile, fry the mushrooms in a frying pan with the remaining plant-based oil until golden, about 10 minutes. Season with the ground kelp and the pepper.

Divide the risotto among serving bowls and top each serve with the crisped golden mushrooms. Garnish each bowl with 1 tablespoon of chopped parsley and serve.

DESSERT

For a large part of my life a wooden spoon has been my weapon of choice. They didn't used to call me Betty Crocker in high school for nothing! I used any excuse I could to bake. I would practically bake sweets for the opening of an envelope. I would whip up brownies, cookies, cakes and slices for everyone to enjoy. Sugar and butter were my best friends. Desserts were so comforting and I found them easy, and people always seemed to admire and love them.

Then at the end of 2012 I realised I needed to change my sugar and butter ways. I let them both go and picked up the stevia and coconut oil instead. Suddenly my world was tipped upside down. I couldn't make a lot of my favourites and, for a while, I honestly thought I had to give up sweets and baking, which didn't make for a very happy Kate! Then I decided to take the challenge and kicked myself into gear. Why shouldn't I be able to have healthy versions of all my favourite desserts?

Here is a collection of some of those favourites. From ice creams and crumble to cakes and puddings, this section covers many of the basics. You might be on a health journey, but enjoying beautiful food is a huge part of that and I hope this section puts a smile on your face, and fills your tummy with nourishing goodness!

BANOFFEE PIE

Serves 12
Prep time: 10 minutes,
    plus 2–3 hours freezing

This recipe is for my sister, a huge lover of banoffee pie – and because she endlessly hassles me to make it for her! This is a much, much healthier version than the original (normally laden with dairy-fat cream and white sugars), and even more delectable. It's easy to make and is a real dinner party winner.

Pie crust
65 g (2¼ oz/⅔ cup) pecans
155 g (5½ oz/1 cup) almonds
165 g (6 oz/1 cup) buckwheat groats*
180 g (6½ oz/2 cups) desiccated coconut
20 medjool dates*, pitted
2 tablespoons coconut oil
½ teaspoon salt
seeds from ½ vanilla bean

Filling
2 tablespoons agar agar*
650 g (1 lb 7 oz/2 cups) Coconut
    'dulce de leche' (page 240)

Topping
2 bananas, sliced
125 g (4½ oz/½ cup) Whipped coconut
    cream (page 239)
50 g (1¾ oz) dark chocolate (at least
    70% cocoa solids)

Place all the pie crust ingredients in a food processor and blitz. Once the mixture starts to come together, tip it into a greased 26.5 cm (10½ in) pie dish and press the mixture up the side and around the edges of the dish. Cover and place in the freezer for 2–3 hours.

For the filling, in a bowl soak the agar agar with 60 ml (2 fl oz/¼ cup) water. Let it sit for 10 minutes. Once thickened, mix it into the coconut dulce until there are no lumps, then pour onto the pie crust base. Place in the refrigerator or freezer for 2–3 hours until set.

Before serving, arrange the banana on top of the pie, smear over the whipped coconut cream and, using a vegetable peeler, shave the dark chocolate on top. Serve and enjoy!

CHOCOLATE AND ALMOND BREAD AND BUTTER PUDDING

Bread and butter pudding was an absolute childhood favourite of mine. When I gave up gluten and became a vegan I said goodbye to this dish and never thought I would be able to eat it again. However, this beauty is not only gluten-free, sugar-free and vegan, it tastes just like the one I used to have when I was younger!

Serves 4
Prep time: 5 minutes
Cooking time: 25 minutes

5 teaspoons coconut oil or Chocolate
  hazelnut butter (see page 227)
10 slices gluten-free bread
250 ml (8½ fl oz/1 cup) soy milk
375 ml (12½ fl oz/1½ cups) coconut cream
1 tablespoon stevia* or xylitol*
60 g (2 oz/½ cup) cornflour (cornstarch)
1 teaspoon lucuma*
1 teaspoon vanilla extract
75 g (2¾ oz) dark chocolate (at least
  70% cocoa solids)
2 tablespoons flaked almonds
2 tablespoons sultanas (golden raisins)

Lightly spread ½ teaspoon coconut oil or chocolate hazelnut butter (for a more chocolatey pudding) on each slice of bread. Cut each slice in half and arrange in a greased oven-safe 24 × 18 cm (9.5 × 7 in) dish.

In a small saucepan over low heat, put the soy milk, coconut cream, stevia, cornflour and lucuma. Whisk until smooth. Add the vanilla and whisk over a gentle heat until the mixture starts to thicken slightly, around 3 minutes.

Preheat the oven to 180°C (350°F).

Pour the custard mixture evenly over the bread slices. Grate over the dark chocolate and sprinkle with the flaked almonds and sultanas. Bake in the oven for 15 minutes or until golden and the custard has become thick. Serve warm or hot.

CARAMEL SLICE

Makes 9–12 squares
Prep time: 25 minutes, plus soaking
    and freezing

This recipe towers over any store-bought caramel slice. The taste is absolutely next level and the perfect balance of saltiness in the slice makes it something that you can eat…then eat a little bit more…and a little bit more. It's also very close to being raw and requires almost no cooking – most of it is done by the food processor.

Cookie base
50 g (1¾ oz/⅓ cup) macadamia nuts
80 g (2¾ oz/½ cup) almonds
80 g (2¾ oz/½ cup) buckwheat groats*
90 g (3 oz/1 cup) desiccated coconut
10 medjool dates*, pitted
1 tablespoon coconut oil
¼ teaspoon salt
seeds from ½ vanilla bean

Caramel filling
14 medjool dates*, pitted
½ teaspoon salt
155 g (5½ oz/1 cup) cashews (soaked in
    water overnight or for a minimum of
    3 hours)
125 g (4½ oz/½ cup) almond butter
160 g (5½ oz/½ cup) Coconut 'dulce de
    leche' (page 240)
60 ml (2 fl oz/¼ cup) coconut cream

Chocolate topping
100 g (3½ oz) melted dark chocolate
    (at least 70% cocoa solids)
1 tablespoon coconut oil
¼ teaspoon salt
35 g (1¼ oz/¼ cup) caramelised buckwheat*

Place all the cookie base ingredients in a food processor and blitz until the mixture is a breadcrumb-like texture and just starting to come together.

Remove the mixture from the food processor and press into the bottom of a 24 × 19 cm (9½ × 7½ in) brownie tin or glass pyrex dish to make a smooth base about 1 cm (½ in) thick. Cover and place in the freezer.

Clean the food processor out with paper towel and then put in all the ingredients for the filling and blitz until a smooth caramel has formed and there are no cashew lumps.

Remove the tin from the freezer and spoon the caramel on top, making sure it is even and smooth. Cover and return to the freezer for 20 minutes.

For the chocolate topping, gently melt the chocolate over a double boiler with the coconut oil and salt.

Remove the slice from the freezer and sprinkle over the caramelised buckwheat. Pour the melted chocolate mix on top and return to the freezer. Once the chocolate has hardened, after about 20 minutes, you're ready to go! You can keep the slice in the freezer for up to 2 weeks. Remove the slice 5 minutes before eating.

CHOCOLATE, MOCHA AND COFFEE LAYER CAKE

This cake was first made for my brother's birthday. Because he is an Ironman and all about health and fitness, I knew I couldn't make him a normal birthday cake. It had to be healthy, and it had to contain two of his favourite things – coffee and chocolate. This was the result, and it's the perfect cake for a celebration!

Serves 6
Prep time: 30 minutes
Cooking time: 30 minutes

Cake base
225 g (8 oz/1½ cups) light buckwheat flour
240 g (8½ oz/1½ cups) brown rice flour
100 g (3½ oz/1 cup) ground almonds
2 teaspoons baking powder
1 teaspoon bicarbonate of soda (baking soda)
*1 tablespoon cacao powder**
*1 tablespoon tapioca flour**
1 teaspoon salt
*105 g (3½ oz/½ cup) stevia**
*125 ml (4 fl oz/½ cup) rice malt syrup**
*250 ml (8½ fl oz/1 cup) plant-based oil**
190 ml (6½ fl oz/¾ cup) coconut oil
*250 ml (8½ fl oz/1 cup) plant-based milk**
*30 g (1 oz) flaxmeal**
125 ml (4 fl oz/½ cup) water

Mocha layer
60 ml (2 fl oz/¼ cup) espresso or cold brew coffee
*30 g (1 oz/¼ cup) cacao powder**

Coffee layer
80 ml (2½ fl oz/⅓ cup) espresso or cold brew coffee
*1 tablespoon stevia**
1 tablespoon buckwheat flour
1 tablespoon brown rice flour

Chocolate layer
*40 g (1½ oz/⅓ cup) cacao powder**

To make the cake base, mix all the ingredients in an electric mixer until combined. Divide the batter into 3 separate bowls.

Preheat the oven to 180°C (350°F).

For the mocha layer, mix the espresso and cacao into the mixture in one of the bowls then pour the mixture into a greased 18.5 cm (7¼ in) cake tin.

For the coffee layer, mix the espresso, stevia, buckwheat flour and brown rice flour into the second bowl and then pour into another greased cake tin.

For the chocolate layer, mix the cacao into the third bowl and pour into another cake tin. Bake the cakes in the oven for 30 minutes or until a skewer comes out clean.

Alternatively, if you only have one cake tin, you just repeat the process 3 times until you have cooked each cake.

Let the cakes cool completely then remove from the tins.

>   >

Filling

1 avocado, stoned
1 banana
30 g (1 oz/¼ cup) cacao powder*
45 g (1½ oz) stevia* (or more if you
  prefer sweeter)

Icing

350 g (12½ oz/2 cups) stevia* icing mix
1 teaspoon vanilla extract
125 ml (4 fl oz/½ cup) coconut cream,
  plus a little extra if needed
30 g (1 oz/¼ cup) cacao powder*

To create the filling, mix the avocado, banana, cacao and stevia and beat with an electric mixer until light and fluffy.

Place the coffee layer cake on a plate and spread the top with the avocado mousse filling. Next, top with the mocha cake, and spread over more mousse, and finally add the chocolate layer on top.

To make the icing, mix all the ingredients, except the cacao, and beat with an electric mixer until combined.

Halve the mixture and stir the cacao into one half. Spread the mixtures onto the cake, a little bit of each at a time (I use a cheese knife), swirling occasionally until the cake is fully coated. Place in the refrigerator until you're ready to serve.

CHOCOLATE GANACHE CAKE

Serves 12
Prep time: 20 minutes, plus soaking
 and 2 hours setting

Chocolate lovers unite! This cake is for anyone who has a love for all things chocolate. Here we have a chocolate base, chocolate filling and a delicious chocolate ganache. This cake only takes about 20 minutes to prepare and it will turn any occasion into a special one!

Base
50 g (1¾ oz) cacao butter*
95 g (3¼ oz/⅔ cup) hazelnuts
80 g (2¾ oz/½ cup) macadamia nuts
30 g (1 oz) cacao powder*
2 tablespoons rice malt syrup*
60 g (2 oz/1 cup) shredded coconut
¼ teaspoon salt

Filling
250 ml (8½ fl oz/1 cup) coconut cream
45 g (1½ oz/½ cup) desiccated coconut
235 g (8½ oz/1½ cups) cashews (soaked in water overnight)
80 g (2¾ oz/½ cup) almonds
60 ml (2 fl oz/¼ cup) rice malt syrup*
30 g (1 oz/¼ cup) cacao powder*
1 teaspoon vanilla extract
6 medjool dates*, pitted
¼ teaspoon salt

Chocolate ganache
200 g (7 oz) dark chocolate (at least 70% cocoa solids)
2 tablespoons coconut cream
1 tablespoon bee pollen* for sprinkling

Place all the base ingredients in a food processor and blitz together until crumb-like. Remove and press into the bottom of a lined 21.5 cm (8½ in) springform tin. Cover and place in the freezer.

For the filling, place all the ingredients in a food processor or blender and blitz until smooth.

Remove the base from the freezer and pour the filling on top of the base, making sure the top is as smooth as possible. Cover and leave to set in the freezer for 2 hours or until hard to the touch.

To make the chocolate ganache, melt the chocolate over a double boiler. Once melted, remove from the heat and mix in the coconut cream. Spread over the top of the cake and sprinkle with bee pollen, serve and enjoy!

This will keep in the freezer for quite a while – just make sure you remove it 10 minutes before serving so it is easier to slice.

COCONUT, FIG AND PISTACHIO 'CHEESECAKE'

This is the cake that first got me some recognition. It was something I came up with that just worked first time. I had it semi-planned in my head before I made it. I chucked everything together in a food processor and it ended up working out perfectly without needing a single tweak! I love this cake, it's definitely a stand out! The filling tastes just like rich white chocolate heavenly goodness, and it's hard to believe you're eating something healthy. Best of all, the recipe is super-easy. This cake has graced many events, it's seen many happy mouths and it's made celebrations of all kinds.

Serves 12 (or more)
Prep time: 10 minutes, plus 2–3 hours
    setting and soaking

Base
160 g (5½ oz/1 cup) macadamia nuts
75 g (2¾ oz/½ cup) pistachio nuts
90 g (3 oz/½ cup) pitted dates
1 teaspoon coconut oil
pinch of salt

Filling
235 g (8½ oz/1½ cups) raw cashews
    (soaked in water overnight)
60 ml (2 fl oz/¼ cup) coconut oil
125 ml (4 fl oz/½ cup) coconut cream
125 g (4½ oz/½ cup) coconut yoghurt
60 ml (2 fl oz/¼ cup) rice malt syrup*
2 tablespoons honey
¼ teaspoon vanilla powder
couple of drops of liquid stevia*

Topping
4–5 figs, chopped
1 tablespoon crushed pistachio nuts
1 tablespoon coconut flakes
1 tablespoon coconut nectar*

First line the bottom of a 21.5 cm (8½ in) springform cake tin with baking paper.

Put all the ingredients for the base in a food processor and process until you have a breadcrumb-like mixture and it begins sticking together.

Press the base mixture firmly into the bottom of the prepared tin and place it in the freezer.

While the base is hardening in the freezer, place all the filling ingredients in a food processor and blitz until creamy and smooth.

Pour the filling on top of the base in the tin and return the cake to the freezer for 2–3 hours.

Remove the now frozen cheesecake from the freezer 20 minutes before you serve it, so it softens slightly.

For the topping, arrange the figs on the top of the cake along with the pistachio nuts and coconut flakes. Drizzle with coconut nectar and you're ready to serve!

Note: You can use any seasonal fruit to top the cake. It works especially well with cherries, plums, or berries.

CHOCOLATE-COATED POPSICLES

Chocolate-coated ice creams just scream summer, fun and enjoyment. These are my take on the milk bar favourite, but you won't be on a sugar high after eating, and you won't be in a heap of regret. These are all good for you!

Makes 4–6 (depending on size of moulds)
Prep time: 30 minutes,
  plus 40 minutes setting

popsicle sticks

Ice cream
*400 ml (13½ fl oz) coconut cream
  (refrigerated)*
125 ml (4 fl oz/½ cup) maple syrup
*155 g (5½ oz/1 cup) cashews (soaked
  in water overnight)*
¼ teaspoon salt
seeds from ½ vanilla bean

Chocolate coating
80 ml (2½ fl oz/⅓ cup) coconut oil
*30 g (1 oz/¼ cup) cacao powder**
*2 tablespoons stevia**
¼ teaspoon sea salt
slivered almonds to garnish

Begin by placing all the ice cream ingredients in a blender and blitz until smooth and creamy. Remove and pour into an ice cream maker, letting it churn for 14 minutes until a beautiful ice cream has formed.

Scoop the ice cream into popsicle moulds, press in the popsicle sticks and place in the freezer for 30 minutes or until frozen.

Mix all the chocolate coating ingredients in a bowl.

Remove the set popsicles from the moulds. Working quickly, dip each ice cream in the chocolate coating – the chocolate will begin to set very quickly on the ice creams as soon as the coconut oil hits the cold ice cream. Sprinkle the almonds on the chocolate before it has set and dunk the popsicle in the chocolate again to coat the almonds.

Return to the freezer until they are ready to eat!

CHOCOLATE CRACKLES

Chocolate crackles never fail to take me back to my childhood. Being at parties nibbling on these was just the best! I knew that even though I had become an adult, I still wanted these in my life, so I created this much MUCH healthier, yet just as tasty, version!

Makes 12–16 crackles
Prep time: 10 minutes,
 plus 20 minutes setting
Cooking time: 10 minutes (optional)

90 g (3 oz/3 cups) puffed brown rice
120 g (4½ oz/2 cups) puffed quinoa*
250 ml (8½ fl oz/1 cup) coconut oil
80 ml (2½ fl oz/⅓ cup) rice malt syrup*
40 g (1½ oz/⅓ cup) carob powder*
90 g (3 oz/1 cup) desiccated coconut
125 g (4½ oz/⅔ cup) xylitol* or stevia*
85 g (3 oz/⅔ cup) cacao powder*
1 teaspoon rose water syrup* (optional)
2 tablespoons slivered pistachio nuts
2 tablespoons rose petals

Preheat the oven to 180°C (350°F), if you want a cooked version of the crackles.

Combine all the ingredients in a bowl and mix together until the puffed brown rice and quinoa are well coated. Spoon into individual paper cases.

Now you have a choice. Either pop the crackles straight into the refrigerator to set if you would prefer a raw version, or cook in the oven for 10 minutes first before placing in the refrigerator!

Leave to set for 20 minutes and eat!

CHOCOLATE MOLTEN PUDDINGS

Serves 4–6
Prep time: 15 minutes
Cooking time: 5–10 minutes

I don't know anyone who doesn't love a gooey, warm chocolate pudding. There is nothing more satisfying than sticking your spoon into the pudding and seeing chocolate lava ooze onto the plate. This was not an easy recipe to master. Most chocolate molten puddings are either 95 per cent chocolate and butter and contain half a dozen eggs, but this recipe is so different in its ingredients, yet just as gorgeous (if not more so). Nobody will believe this is high in antioxidants and good for you, but I assure you, it is!

4–6 teaspoons vegan butter for greasing
175 g (6 oz/1 cup) grain-sweetened
  chocolate chips*
2 tablespoons coconut oil
80 ml (2½ fl oz/⅓ cup) plant-based milk*
130 g (4½ oz/1 cup) buckwheat flour
1 teaspoon baking powder
½ teaspoon salt
60 g (2 oz/½ cup) cacao powder*,
  plus 1 extra tablespoon for dusting
210 g (7½ oz/1 cup) stevia*
250 ml (8½ fl oz/1 cup) soy milk
80–120 ml (2½–4 fl oz) coconut cream
  to serve

Grease 4–6 ramekins with 1 teaspoon vegan butter.

Place the ramekins on baking paper, and draw a circle around them. Cut out the shapes and press the paper into the bottom of each ramekin. Set aside.

Put the chocolate chips, coconut oil and plant-based milk in a double boiler. Gently heat until the chocolate has melted. Stir until smooth, remove from the heat and set aside.

Preheat the oven to 180°C (350°F).

In another bowl, put the flour, baking powder, salt, cacao and stevia. Stir together. Add the soy milk and mix until combined. Gently fold in the chocolate mixture.

Divide the mixture into the prepared ramekins and place on a baking tray. Bake in the oven for 5–10 minutes until the edges and top are just cooked – you still want the middle to be gooey as it will keep cooking once removed from the oven.

When ready to serve, gently run a knife around the edge of the ramekins to loosen the puddings, then turn them out onto a plate and serve with coconut cream and a light dusting of cacao.

JAM DONUT BALLS

Makes about 16 donuts
Prep time: 15 minutes,
   plus 75 minutes rising
Cooking time: 20 minutes

This recipe is dedicated to my mum, who has an absolute love of donut balls. I cannot count the times I have caught her with cinnamon-sugar fingers after she has been to the shopping centre. I must admit I am also very partial to a good jam donut, so I present to you a much more nutritious version – although still keep this as just an every-so-often treat!

250 ml (8½ fl oz/1 cup) plant-based milk*,
   lukewarm
60 g (2 oz) coconut sugar*, plus extra
   for rolling
8 g (¼ oz) dry yeast
240 g (8½ oz/1½ cups) superfine brown
   rice flour or plain gluten-free flour
195 g (7 oz/1½ cups) buckwheat flour
1 teaspoon salt
500 ml (17 fl oz/2 cups) plant-based oil*
160 g (5½ oz/½ cup) Berry chia jam
   (page 219)

In a bowl, combine the warmed milk, coconut sugar and yeast. Whisk and then set aside for 10 minutes or until frothy. If it doesn't froth, discard it and start again.

In another bowl, combine the flours and salt. Add the yeasted milk and stir to combine, until you have a dough-like consistency.

Turn the dough out onto a lightly floured surface, knead for 5 minutes and then place in a lightly oiled bowl. Place the bowl in a warm spot and leave to rise for 45 minutes.

Remove the dough from the bowl, knead again for 5 minutes then break into about 16 individual balls. Set aside again in a warm place to rise for 30 minutes.

In a medium saucepan on medium–high heat, heat the plant-based oil. The oil is hot enough when you drop in a small bit of dough and it bubbles immediately.

Carefully drop in the donut balls, 2–3 at a time, and cook for 3–4 minutes each until golden. Roll the donuts immediately in coconut sugar and set aside.

Once all the donuts are cooked, using a piping (icing) bag, fill each donut with jam, serve and enjoy!

CHOCOLATE, ROSEMARY AND OLIVE OIL CAKE

All right, this cake is definitely a winner to bring out for afternoon tea. It has a great texture, beautiful complementary flavours and its beauty is something else! This cake never fails to bring me happiness, and I hope the chocolatey hit and herbs do the same for you.

Serves 12
Prep time: 15 minutes
Cooking time: 30 minutes

195 g (7 oz/1½ cups) light buckwheat flour
240 g (8½ oz/1½ cups) brown rice flour
100 g (3½ oz/1 cup) ground almonds
2 teaspoons baking powder
1 teaspoon bicarbonate of soda
   (baking soda)
1 tablespoon cacao powder*
1 tablespoon tapioca flour*
1 teaspoon salt
105 g (3½ oz/½ cup) stevia*
250 ml (8½ fl oz/1 cup) olive oil
190 ml (6½ fl oz/¾ cup) coconut oil
250 ml (8½ fl oz/1 cup) plant-based milk*
125 ml (4 fl oz/½ cup) rice malt syrup*
30 g (1 oz) flaxmeal*
100 g (3½ oz) dark chocolate (at least
   70% cocoa solids), chopped into
   rough pieces
leaves from 2 rosemary sprigs

Icing
75 g (2¾ oz) dark chocolate (at least
   70% cocoa solids)
2 tablespoons coconut oil
1 tablespoon coconut cream

Preheat the oven to 180°C (350°F).

Put the flours, ground almonds, baking powder, bicarbonate of soda, cacao, tapioca, salt and stevia in an electric mixer. Mix on medium speed for 2 minutes with the whisk attachment and then add the olive oil, coconut oil and milk and mix again. Once everything is combined, add the rice malt syrup, flaxmeal and 125 ml (4 fl oz/½ cup) water and mix for 2 minutes or until everything is well combined.

Fold in the chocolate pieces and the rosemary leaves.

Transfer to a well-greased 23 cm (9 in) ring (bundt) tin and bake in the oven for 30 minutes or until a skewer comes out clean.

Remove from the oven and allow the cake to cool completely before removing from the tin.

For the icing, put the chocolate and coconut oil in a double boiler over low heat. Once melted, remove from the heat and mix in the coconut cream.

Drizzle the icing over the cake and place in the refrigerator for 5 minutes to set. Slice and serve!

COCONUT ICE CREAM 6 WAYS

Ice cream and I go together like trees and the woods. I could eat ice cream for breakfast, lunch, dinner and dessert, summer or winter – in other words, there is no time I don't feel like ice cream. This is one of my classic ice cream recipes that I have adapted into different flavours. Just 15 minutes in the ice cream maker and you're done!

Serves 4
Prep time: 20 minutes

For best results, keep the coconut cream in the refrigerator for a few hours or overnight before making the ice cream.

Place all the ingredients for the ice cream flavour of your choice in a blender and blitz until smooth.

Transfer the mixture to an ice cream maker and churn for 15 minutes or until frozen.

Eat immediately or transfer to a container and store in the freezer for up to 1 month. If not eating immediately, make sure you take it out of the freezer for 5–10 minutes to soften slightly before scooping!

BERRY ICE CREAM

800 ml (27 fl oz) coconut cream
165 g (6 oz/¾ cup) mixed berries
125 ml (4 fl oz/½ cup) rice malt syrup*
1 tablespoon maple syrup
pinch of salt

MANGO ICE CREAM

800 ml (27 fl oz) coconut cream
240 g (8½ oz/¾ cup) mango pieces
125 ml (4 fl oz/½ cup) rice malt syrup*
1 tablespoon maple syrup
zest of 1 lime
3 mint leaves
pinch of salt

>

CHOCOLATE ICE CREAM

800 ml (27 fl oz) coconut cream
60 g (2 oz/½ cup) cacao powder*
125 ml (4 fl oz/½ cup) rice malt syrup*
1 tablespoon maple syrup
pinch of salt

ESPRESSO ICE CREAM

800 ml (27 fl oz) coconut cream
125 ml (4 fl oz/½ cup) espresso/cold
  brew coffee
125 ml (4 fl oz/½ cup) rice malt syrup*
1 tablespoon maple syrup
pinch of salt

CHOC HAZELNUT ICE CREAM

800 ml (27 fl oz) coconut cream
30 g (1 oz/¼ cup) cacao powder*
60 g (2 oz/¼ cup) Chocolate hazelnut
  butter (page 227)
125 ml (4 fl oz/½ cup) rice malt syrup*
1 tablespoon maple syrup
pinch of salt

VANILLA ICE CREAM

800 ml (27 fl oz) coconut cream
125 ml (4 fl oz/½ cup) rice malt syrup*
1 tablespoon maple syrup
2 teaspoons vanilla extract
pinch of salt

FRUIT CUSTARD TARTS

Serves 4
Prep time: 10 minutes,
  plus 2 hours freezing
Cooking time: 10 minutes

Buying a fruit custard tart from the bakery is one of my favourite memories from childhood. There was always something so amazing about biting into perfect fruit and soft custard.

Pie crust
155 g (5½ oz/1 cup) almonds
65 g (2¼ oz/⅔ cup) walnuts
140 g (5 oz/1 cup) buckwheat groats*
180 g (6½ oz/2 cups) desiccated coconut
20 medjool dates*, pitted
2 tablespoons coconut oil
½ teaspoon salt
seeds from ½ vanilla bean

Custard
400 ml (13½ fl oz) tin coconut cream
1 tablespoon stevia*
60 ml (2 fl oz/¼ cup) water
45 g (1½ oz) cornflour (cornstarch)
½ teaspoon vanilla powder (or 1 teaspoon
  vanilla extract)
1 tablespoon mesquite* or lucuma*
  for extra flavour (optional)

To serve
110 g (4 oz/½ cup) fresh berries
lime zest (optional)

Place all the pie crust ingredients in a food processor and blitz until the mixture starts to form a dough.

Press the dough with your fingers into 4 individual dishes or tart cases and place in the refrigerator or freezer for 2 hours.

To make the custard, put all the ingredients in a saucepan over medium heat and whisk until the custard becomes thick, about 5 minutes.

When ready to serve, spoon the filling into the tart cases and sprinkle with the berries and lime zest, if using.

LEMON TART

Serves 12
Prep time: 25 minutes,
    plus 2–3 hours setting

I don't know many people who would say no to a good slice of lemon tart. Usually laden with egg yolks, cream and white sugar, the humble lemon tart can be a bit of a health nut's nightmare! However, this recipe is quite the opposite – it's delicious, simple and just as satisfying as the classic version.

Tart crust
50 g (1¾ oz/⅓ cup) macadamia nuts
115 g (4 oz/¾ cup) almonds
125 g (4½ oz/¾ cup) buckwheat groats*
115 g (4 oz/1¼ cups) desiccated coconut
12 medjool dates*, pitted
2 tablespoons coconut oil
zest of 1 lemon
¼ teaspoon salt
seeds from ½ vanilla bean

Lemon filling
4 teaspoons agar agar flakes*
125 ml (4 fl oz/½ cup) lemon juice
125 ml (4 fl oz/½ cup) maple syrup
125 ml (4 fl oz/½ cup) coconut cream
2 teaspoons lemon zest
60 ml (2 fl oz/¼ cup) rice malt syrup*
1 teaspoon lucuma*
4 teaspoons kuzu*, ground into a powder
2 tablespoons cornflour (cornstarch)

To serve
*coconut cream or Coconut ice cream
    (page 179)*

Begin by placing all the tart crust ingredients in a food processor and blitz for 5 minutes or until you have a nice moist crumb-like texture.

Press the mixture into the base and up the side of a 26.5 cm (10½ in) large pie dish, and place in the refrigerator or freezer.

For the lemon filling, place the agar agar in 80 ml (2½ fl oz/⅓ cup) water to soak for 20 minutes and set aside.

In a saucepan over medium heat, put the lemon juice, maple syrup, coconut cream, lemon zest, rice malt syrup and lucuma. Whisk the ground kuzu into the mixture. Add the agar agar and cornflour and keep whisking for 1–2 minutes, but take it off the heat before it thickens.

Pour the filling into the refrigerated tart crust and place the tart into the refrigerator to set for 2–3 hours.

When ready to serve, slice the tart and serve with coconut cream or a scoop of coconut ice cream.

PANNA COTTA WITH ALMOND BRITTLE AND BERRY SAUCE

This is a dish with a wow factor. Although panna cotta is one of the easiest desserts to make, there is something fancy about it. The almond brittle is one of the best toffees you will ever eat and, mixed together with a spoonful of the creamy panna cotta and berry sauce, you will be transported to another world!

Serves 4
Prep time: 5 minutes, plus 2–3 hours setting, plus cooling
Cooking time: 30 minutes

Panna cotta
*1 tablespoon agar agar flakes**
500 ml (17 fl oz/2 cups) coconut milk
*250 ml (8½ fl oz/1 cup) soy or other plant-based milk**
2 tablespoons maple syrup
1 teaspoon vanilla extract

Almond brittle
80 g (2¾ oz/½ cup) chopped/crushed almonds
*60 ml (2 fl oz/¼ cup) rice malt syrup**
*45 g (1½ oz) coconut sugar**

Berry sauce
155 g (5½ oz/1 cup) frozen berries
*2 tablespoons rice malt syrup**
*1 tablespoon stevia**

For the panna cotta, soak the agar agar in the coconut milk and plant-based milk in a saucepan and let sit for 10 minutes. Add the remaining panna cotta ingredients and warm the mixture over medium heat for 5 minutes or until it has thickened slightly. Remove from the heat and pour into 4 moulds. Cover and leave in the refrigerator to set for 2–3 hours.

Preheat the oven to 180°C (350°F) and line a baking tray with baking paper.

For the almond brittle, scatter the almonds on the baking tray. Pour over the rice malt syrup and sprinkle on the coconut sugar. Cook for 10 minutes, or until the rice malt and coconut sugar are bubbling and there are no big lumps of coconut sugar. Remove from the oven and set aside for about 30 minutes to cool down and harden.

For the berry sauce, in a small saucepan over medium heat, combine all the ingredients. Cook until most of the liquid has evaporated, about 10 minutes, and remove from the heat.

To assemble, quickly dunk the panna cotta moulds in boiling water and then turn them out, or gently go around the outside of the moulds with a butter knife. Top the pannacotta with the berry sauce and a few pieces of almond brittle and serve.

APPLE CRUMBLE WITH COCONUT CUSTARD

Serves 4–6
Prep time: 25 minutes
Cooking time: 30 minutes

When winter hits, there is something very comforting about stewed fruits and warm desserts. Apple crumble with custard ticks all the winter comfort food boxes. However the butter, kilojoule (calorie) content and refined sugar found in the standard version of this dessert will often lead to winter weight being stacked on. So I decided to create my own vegan, refined sugar-free and butter-free version – to satisfy my own winter comfort food cravings, and to also cater for my family's love of puddings. If I said that this crumble and custard wasn't very good I would be lying. Just try it for yourself and see what you think. I can almost guarantee you won't go back to the original after this.

Filling
2 kg (4 lb 6 oz) organic apples (preferably green and peeled, but you can leave the skin on), chopped into thick slices or however you like them
juice of 1 orange
1 teaspoon stevia*
10 medjool dates*, pitted and chopped into quarters
1 tablespoon coconut oil

Crumble
2 tablespoons desiccated coconut
1 tablespoon coconut flour
handful of rolled (porridge) gluten-free oats or quinoa flakes*
25 g (1 oz/¼ cup) flaked almonds
20 g (¾ oz/⅓ cup) puffed quinoa*
50 g (1¾ oz/⅓ cup) pepitas (pumpkin seeds), preferably activated
35 g (1¼ oz/¼ cup) caramelised buckwheat* or plain activated buckwheat
2 tablespoons coconut sugar*
60 ml (2 fl oz/¼ cup) coconut oil

First, for the filling, place the apples in a medium saucepan on low heat with the orange juice, stevia, dates and coconut oil. Let the mixture simmer for 10–15 minutes, occasionally stirring, until the apples have softened and absorbed all the liquid. Remove from the heat and set aside.

Preheat the oven to 180°C (350°F).

Next, put all the crumble ingredients, except the coconut oil, in a mixing bowl and stir to combine. Add the coconut oil to the mixture and rub it in with your fingertips. Once a crumb-like consistency is formed, or all the ingredients are coated in the oil, you're ready to go.

Place the stewed apples in a 24 × 18 cm (9½ × 7 in) baking dish (or 4–6 individual 7.5 cm/3 in ramekins) and top with the crumble mixture. Cook in the oven for 15 minutes, until the top is nice and golden.

>

>

Custard

1 tablespoon stevia*
400 ml (13½ fl oz) tin coconut cream
45 g (1½ oz) cornflour (cornstarch)
½ teaspoon vanilla powder or 1 teaspoon
   vanilla extract
1 tablespoon mesquite* or lucuma*, for extra
   flavour (optional)

While your crumble is in the oven, make the custard. Place the stevia and 60 ml (2 fl oz/ ¼ cup) water in a saucepan over medium heat. Bring the water to the boil and remove from the heat once the stevia has dissolved.

Place the remaining custard ingredients in a pitcher or mixing bowl and whisk until combined and smooth – we don't want any lumps! Add this mixture to the stevia and water mixture in the saucepan and return to a low heat. Whisk the mixture over the heat until thickened and a custard texture is achieved. (You can make the custard in advance, place it in a pitcher or bowl, cover and set aside in the refrigerator. It will last a couple of days – if you can resist it for that long!)

Once the crumble is cooked, remove it from the oven. Serve it with a dollop of custard, eat and enjoy!

Note: You can also use half pears and half apples if desired. Pears also add a great taste.

RASPBERRY ICE CREAM SANDWICHES

These are absolute little delights to make and eat. They're perfect to give to kids (or adults) and they are fuss-free!

Serves 6
Prep time: 30 minutes, plus
   20–30 minutes freezing
Cooking time: 5–10 minutes

Sugar cookies

195 g (7 oz/1½ cups) buckwheat flour, plus extra for dusting
160 g (5½ oz/1 cup) brown rice flour
160 g (5½ oz/¾ cup) stevia* or xylitol*
½ teaspoon salt
1 teaspoon baking powder
80 ml (2½ fl oz/⅓ cup) coconut oil
170 ml (5½ fl oz/⅔ cup) plant-based milk*
2 teaspoons vanilla essence

Ice cream

800 ml (27 fl oz) coconut cream
125 ml (4 fl oz/½ cup) rice malt syrup*
2 tablespoons maple syrup
pinch of salt
1 teaspoon vanilla extract
90 g (3 oz/¾ cup) frozen raspberries

Begin by putting all the ice cream ingredients, except the raspberries, in a blender and mixing until smooth. Transfer to an ice cream maker. Start churning and, after about 15 minutes, when the ice cream begins to thicken, add the frozen raspberries. Transfer the ice cream to a lined square 23 cm (9 in) brownie tin. Flatten the ice cream to about 7.5 cm (3 in) thick and allow to freeze for 20–30 minutes.

For the sugar cookies, place all the ingredients in an electric mixer and beat on medium setting for 5 minutes or until a dough has formed. On a well-floured surface, roll out the mixture to 5 mm (¼ in) thick, adding more flour as needed.

Preheat the oven to 180°C (350°F) and line a baking tray with baking paper.

Cut out twelve 9 cm (3½ in) circles and place on the baking tray and cook for 10 minutes. Remove from the oven and allow to cool completely on the tray.

Using a large round cookie cutter, cut rounds out of the ice cream the same size as the pastry, and then sandwich the ice cream round between 2 of the shortcrust rounds. Place the ice cream sandwiches back in the freezer until ready to eat.

SWEET POTATO BROWNIES WITH CHICKPEA COOKIE DOUGH

Serves 9–12
Prep time: 15 minutes
Cooking time: 45 minutes

First, these are my favourite brownies ever. Second, I love the cookie dough topping even more. I often have some of the dough in the refrigerator ready to roll into balls, or to use as a filling for truffles when I need a little sweet fix. This combination is a game changer in the brownie world. It is perfect for kids – getting in the nutrients from both the sweet potato and chickpeas (garbanzo beans), without them even realising they are eating something healthy!

Brownies
*2 sweet potatoes, peeled and chopped
    into 5 cm (2 in) pieces
14 medjool dates*, pitted
70 g (2½ oz/⅔ cup) ground almonds
65 g (2¼ oz/½ cup) buckwheat flour
1 teaspoon baking powder
40 g (1½ oz) cacao powder*
60 ml (2 fl oz/¼ cup) maple syrup
½ teaspoon salt
125 ml (4 fl oz/½ cup) plant-based milk**

Cookie dough topping
*400 g (14 oz) tinned chickpeas (garbanzo
    beans), drained and rinsed
60 ml (2 fl oz/¼ cup) maple syrup
80 g (2¾ oz) almond butter
¼ teaspoon salt
90 g (3 oz/½ cup) grain-sweetened
    chocolate chips**

Preheat the oven to 180°C (350°F).

Begin by steaming the sweet potatoes for 10–15 minutes, or until soft. Transfer to a food processor or blender and blitz with the remaining brownie ingredients.

Once a smooth mixture has formed, pour the mixture into a lined or greased square 23 cm (9 in) brownie tin and bake for 20–30 minutes or until a skewer comes out clean. Remove from the oven and allow to cool.

To make the chickpea cookie dough, place all the ingredients, except the chocolate chips, in a food processor and blitz until a beautiful cookie dough-like mix has formed. Fold through the chocolate chips.

Smooth the cookie dough topping over the brownies in the tin and place in the refrigerator until ready to serve. Cut into pieces before serving.

DRINKS

*One of the first things on my mind when
I wake up in the morning is, 'Which juice
am I going to make?'. Then, when it comes
to morning tea, or after a workout, I wonder
what smoothie to make. If I begin to feel run
down, sluggish or lethargic I go straight into
the kitchen to hydrate myself with water, fresh
juice, a smoothie or a herbal tea.*

*Drinking and staying hydrated is always
my first priority when it comes to my health —
drinking enough liquid to ensure my body
and mind are working the way they should,
absorbing nutrients I wouldn't be able to get
from food.*

*I have never been an alcohol drinker. At
parties in high school I was normally there
with a 6-pack of juice boxes in my hand.
I definitely went through a very short-lived
teenage partying stage though. Even then
I knew that the next day the only thing that
would make me feel better was to get a juice in
me, to give me the most nutrients as quickly as
possible to get me feeling normal again!*

*I have also included some non-alcoholic
cocktails, as maybe you're like me and prefer
the drink in your hand to not be alcoholic, but
you still want something delicious.*

*Drinking is also a way of relaxing, even just
for 5 minutes; sitting down with a cup of tea
and rebooting the mind. It's another form of
meditation and a great excuse to take a load
off, exhale and re-energise.*

ANTI-AGEING GREEN SMOOTHIE

Serves 2
Prep time: 5 minutes

This humble green smoothie is so packed with anti-ageing foods that you will practically turn into a teenager after drinking it! OK, that is not true, but it will do all the right things for your body, and help turn back the clock. Think good fats, fresh fruit and leafy greens with the best produce to make your body feel great.

2 bananas
½ avocado
80 g (2¾ oz/½ cup) blueberries
4 kale leaves
20 g (¾ oz/⅓ cup) broccoli florets
*2 tablespoons hemp seeds**
1 tablespoon olive oil
*375 ml (12½ fl oz/1½ cups) plant-based milk**
*1 tablespoon lucuma**

Place all the ingredients in a blender and process until smooth. Serve immediately.

MANGO AND TURMERIC LASSI

There is nothing like a lassi to serve with curries, or to simply drink on its own. This little lassi is perfect to whip out when you feel a cold or flu coming on.

Serves 2
Prep time: 5 minutes

3 frozen mango cheeks
*250 g (9 oz/1 cup) coconut
   yoghurt*
*375 ml (12½ fl oz/1½ cups)
   plant-based milk**
½ teaspoon ground cardamom
½ teaspoon turmeric
small pinch of salt
1 tablespoon rice malt syrup*

Place all the ingredients in a blender and process until smooth. Serve immediately.

HANGOVER-FREE COCKTAILS

I am not a big drinker (if ever) but I do like to enjoy myself when other people are consuming alcohol. These drinks are my favourite non-alcoholic cocktails, which are sure to be a hit at any party.

Each juice serves 2
Prep time: 15 minutes

PINEAPPLE, MINT AND LUCUMA

¼ pineapple, peeled and chopped
5 g (¼ oz/¼ cup) mint leaves, plus extra
 to serve
2 oranges, peeled and chopped
1 teaspoon lucuma*
lime wedges to serve
mint sprig to serve

Feed the pineapple, mint and oranges through a juicer. Stir the lucuma into the liquid and pour into glasses. Serve with a wedge of lime and a sprig of mint.

CUCUMBER, MINT AND LIME

1 cucumber, plus slices to garnish
1 lime, skin removed
5 g (¼ oz/¼ cup) mint, plus leaves to garnish
soda water (club soda) to top

Feed the cucumber, lime and mint through a juicer. Serve over ice with extra mint, a splash of soda water and extra cucumber slices. Serve immediately.

>

APPLE AND GINGER

4 apples, chopped, plus extra slices to serve
½ lime, skin removed
5 cm (2 in) piece fresh ginger
1 teaspoon coconut sugar*
lemon wedges to serve

Feed the apples, lime and ginger through a juicer. Mix in the coconut sugar and serve over ice with apple slices and lemon wedges.

WATERMELON MOCKITO

¼ watermelon, peeled and chopped
½ cucumber, chopped
½ lime, skin removed
1 cm (½ in) piece ginger
5 g (¼ oz/¼ cup) mint leaves
soda water (club soda) to top

Feed the watermelon, cucumber, lime and ginger through a juicer. At the bottom of your glasses, place some ice and the mint. Add the watermelon liquid and muddle together with the mint. Top with soda water for a more sparkling drink.

METABOLISM-BOOSTING BERRY SMOOTHIE

This is my favourite drink, especially if I have eaten something greasy. It kicks your body back into gear and helps to get your metabolism moving, while also fighting free radicals with a huge burst of antioxidants. It's also filled with fibre!

Serves 2
Prep time: 5 minutes

1 tablespoon matcha*
½ teaspoon cinnamon
80 g (2¾ oz/½ cup) blueberries
30 g (1 oz/¼ cup) raspberries
30 g (1 oz/¼ cup) blackberries
1 teaspoon apple cider vinegar
375 ml (12½ fl oz/1½ cups)
  almond milk
1 banana, frozen
¼ avocado
1 teaspoon almond butter
1 teaspoon psyllium husks*

Combine all the ingredients in a blender and process until smooth. Serve in 2 large glasses. Enjoy immediately.

COLD-PRESSED JUICES

Each juice
Serves 2
Prep time: 15 minutes

For each juice, feed the ingredients through your juicer, pour into glasses and enjoy the beautiful pick-me-up!

I am a juice fanatic. I have to drink a juice first thing in the morning, as a pick-me-up in the afternoon and often one just before dinner. There is something so rewarding and nourishing about being able to take beautiful fresh produce and turn it into a delicious liquid. I use juices as my medicine. Knowing I can't possibly eat all the ingredients to get the nutrients, I juice it so I get a big nutrient burst in a glass. You know there are no hidden sugars or preservatives when you make juice at home and you can go wild with combinations! The following combinations are a great start into the juice world and just brilliant in flavour.

ANTIOXIDANT JUICE

80 g (2¾ oz/½ cup) blueberries
60 g (2 oz/½ cup) raspberries
75 g (2¾ oz/½ cup) strawberries
1 small beetroot (beet), chopped
1 red plum, stoned and halved
2 red apples, chopped
¼ cucumber, chopped
5 g (¼ oz/¼ cup) mint leaves

MORNING JUICE

1 orange, skin removed
1 peach, stoned
¼ pineapple, peeled and chopped
1 carrot, chopped
1 green apple, chopped
2 celery stalks, chopped
2.5 cm (1 in) piece fresh ginger

ALKALISING GREEN JUICE

2 green apples, chopped
1 cucumber, chopped
1 celery stalk, chopped
2 cos (romaine) lettuce leaves, washed
3 kale leaves, washed
½ lemon, skin on
2.5 cm (1 in) piece fresh ginger

WATERMELON DRAGON JUICE

2 large pieces watermelon, chopped
1 red dragon fruit*, peeled
½ cucumber, chopped
1 lime
5 g (¼ oz/¼ cup) mint

CLOCKWISE FROM LEFT:
MORNING JUICE,
ANTIOXIDANT JUICE,
ALKALISING GREEN JUICE

CLOCKWISE FROM LEFT:
CHOCOLATE HAZELNUT MILK,
COCONUT CASHEW MILK,
ALMOND ESPRESSO MILK

NUT MILKS

Each recipe makes 1 litre
(34 fl oz/4 cups) milk
Prep time: 10 minutes

To make the basic nut milk, place the
nuts and filtered water in a blender.
Blitz for up to 2–3 minutes.

Strain through a nut bag into a bottle
or bowl, and keep stored in the refrigerator.

For the other nut milks, simply blitz all
the ingredients in a blender and pour
into a bottle to keep in the refrigerator
for 2–3 days.

Note: Nut bags are available from health food stores
and some greengrocers.

*Nut milks are extremely cost-efficient and delicious
to make at home. They have a very creamy and
beautiful taste and it's incredibly satisfying to
make such a basic thing yourself. Here is my very
basic nut milk recipe, along with a few of my
favourite combinations.*

BASIC NUT MILK

140 g (5 oz/1 cup) nuts of choice
(soaked overnight in water)
1 litre (34 fl oz/4 cups) filtered water

CHOCOLATE HAZELNUT MILK

1 litre (34 fl oz/4 cups) Basic nut milk
made with hazelnuts (see left)
2 tablespoons cacao
¼ teaspoon sea salt
1–2 tablespoons stevia*
½ tablespoon coconut oil

ALMOND ESPRESSO MILK

1 litre (34 fl oz/4 cups) Basic nut milk
made with almonds (see above)
1–2 shots espresso or 125 ml (4 fl oz/½ cup)
cold brew coffee
2 medjool dates*, pitted
¼ teaspoon sea salt
½ tablespoon coconut oil

COCONUT CASHEW MILK

1 litre (34 fl oz/4 cups) Basic nut milk
made with cashews (see above left)
¼ teaspoon sea salt
125 ml (4 fl oz/½ cup) coconut milk
1 tablespoon stevia*
½ tablespoon coconut oil

HOMEMADE CHAI

I am a huge chai enthusiast. It makes me feel relaxed and at ease. The spices warm my belly and it's so pleasurable to consume. I love chai hot or cold, so here are two ways to have my favourite spiced tea.

Serves 4
Prep time: 5 minutes
Cooking time: 15 minutes

Chai spice
60 ml (2 fl oz/¼ cup) black tea
3 cinnamon sticks
6 star anise
6 cardamom pods
8 cloves
½ teaspoon ground nutmeg
¼ teaspoon ground ginger
1½ tablespoons cacao powder*
seeds from 1 vanilla bean
50 g (1¾ oz/¼ cup) coconut sugar*
    or rice malt syrup*

Creamer milk
500 ml (17 fl oz/2 cups) coconut cream
500 ml (17 fl oz/2 cups) soy milk

For iced chai, begin by mixing all the chai spice ingredients together with 500 ml (17 fl oz/2 cups) water in a saucepan. Bring to the boil over medium heat and then reduce to low and let simmer for 15 minutes (up to 30 minutes if you want a stronger chai taste). Remove from the heat, strain and place the liquid in a bottle.

For the creamer, mix the coconut cream and soy milk together.

Pour the chai into a glass filled with ice, and top with the desired amount of creamer.

Alternatively, for a warm milk chai, simply omit the water with the chai spice ingredients and use the creamer instead. Warm the chai and milk up in a saucepan for 10 minutes or until the milk has turned a beautiful caramel colour, strain and enjoy.

CONDIMENTS

My refrigerator and cupboard shelves are packed with condiments. I find they can add so much new life to a dish – they can transform it into something new or even be used as the base of a dish. The following recipes are a small collection of some of my favourite condiments that I always have made on hand. From sauces to jams, from cheeses to pickles, from savoury to sweet, all of these condiments are very easy to create from scratch and will add a huge flavour change to your meals. It's time to say no to store-bought and yes to homemade and see the endless nutritional benefits from doing so. These condiments are my secret weapons in the kitchen and always provide me with inspiration to create.

BERRY CHIA JAM

Makes about 630 g
 (1 lb 6 oz/2 cups)
Prep time: 5 minutes
Cooking time: 5 minutes

To say that I love this jam would be an understatement. Spread it on toast, dollop it onto yoghurt, eat it from the jar or use it in your cooking. This jam is packed with omega-3s thanks to the beautiful chia seeds, and it's simply amazing to eat!

*440 g (15½ oz/2 cups)
 mixed berries
2–3 tablespoons stevia*
juice of 1 lemon
1 tablespoon water
1 tablespoon rice malt syrup*
1 teaspoon vanilla extract
 (optional)
60 g (2 oz/½ cup) chia seeds**

Place all the ingredients, except the chia seeds, in a small saucepan over medium heat and let simmer until the stevia has dissolved, about 2 minutes. Remove from the heat, add the chia seeds, stir and place in a sterilised jar.

Place in the refrigerator to set overnight and enjoy! The jam keeps in the refrigerator for up to 3 weeks.

CASHEW 'GOAT'S' CHEESE

Makes about 250 g (9 oz/1 cup)
Prep time: 15 minutes, plus
  2–3 hours setting, plus
  soaking time for cashews

My love for cheese extends beyond the normal dairy cheeses, and I have moved on to a love of artisan nut cheeses. This cashew 'goat's' cheese is something that I use almost every day. It's perfect spread on a piece of toast with avocado, crumbled over a salad or used to make a rich, creamy cheesy sauce. This cheese is well balanced in flavour and is a must for anyone with a love of cheese, but who prefers a healthier option.

310 g (11 oz/2 cups) raw
  cashews, soaked in water
  overnight, drained
1 teaspoon salt
2 tablespoons coconut oil
60 ml (2 fl oz/¼ cup) water
juice of 1 lemon
1 teaspoon savoury yeast
  flakes*

Place all the ingredients in a food processor or blender and blitz until the mixture is smooth.

Roll the cheese into a log shape or ball using a piece of muslin (cheesecloth) or baking paper. Place in the refrigerator for 2–3 hours to chill and set.

This will keep in a container in the refrigerator for 1–2 weeks and will keep in the freezer for 1 month.

MACADAMIA 'RICOTTA' CHEESE

Makes about 250 g (9 oz/1 cup)
Prep time: 10 minutes, plus
  soaking time for nuts

This is another cheese that can be used across a smorgasbord of dishes. It's delicious on its own, it's perfect to mix into risottos or pasta dishes, is amazing in sweets and is generally brilliant to use as a substitute for the dairy version.

320 g (11½ oz/2 cups) raw macadamia nuts, soaked in water overnight, drained
2 tablespoons coconut oil
juice of 1 lemon
1 teaspoon salt
1 teaspoon savoury yeast flakes*

Place the macadamia nuts in a food processor with the coconut oil, 2 tablespoons water and the lemon juice and blitz until smooth. Add the salt and savoury yeast flakes. Keep blending until the cheese is as smooth as you like.

Store it in a container in the refrigerator for up to 1 week.

TURMERIC BUTTER

Prep time: 5–10 minutes
Makes about 250 g (9 oz/1 cup)

OK, OK, OK. I really, really love this spread. It's buttery, it's packed with nutrients and it's SO perfect as a butter replacement to smear on toast or use in curries, stir-fries, soups or you name it! I constantly have a jar of this on the go in my house, sneaking it into my family's food wherever possible.

155 g (5½ oz/1 cup) raw
  cashew nuts
155 g (5½ oz/1 cup) brazil nuts
60 ml (2 fl oz/¼ cup)
  coconut oil
1 teaspoon maca*
½ teaspoon salt
2 teaspoons turmeric powder

Place all the ingredients in a food processor and blitz until a smooth butter has formed (this will take about 5–10 minutes). Place in a sterilised jar and keep in the refrigerator for up to 2 weeks.

ALMOND, BRAZIL
AND CASHEW
(ABC) BUTTER

NUT BUTTERS

Each makes about 250 g (9 oz/1 cup)
Prep time: 12 minutes

For each nut butter, place the ingredients in a food processor or blender and blitz for 10 minutes or until smooth. Add extra stevia to the chocolate hazelnut butter if not quite sweet enough.

I am one of those people who could eat nut butter by the spoonful. It's a high-protein snack that I am either stuffing into a beautiful medjool date, spreading on a banana or toast, putting in muesli (granola) bars or using somewhere in my cooking. These nut butters are my favourite three to have on hand. They are simple to create, delicious and will give you energy. These nut butters store for up to 2 weeks in the refrigerator.

ALMOND, BRAZIL AND CASHEW (ABC) BUTTER

115 g (4 oz/¾ cup) almonds
115 g (4 oz/¾ cup) brazil nuts
115 g (4 oz/¾ cup) cashew nuts
¼ teaspoon sea salt

PISTACHIO, ALMOND AND CARDAMOM BUTTER

130 g (4½ oz/1 cup) pistachio nuts
80 g (2¾ oz/½ cup) almonds
¼ teaspoon sea salt
¼ teaspoon cardamom

CHOCOLATE HAZELNUT BUTTER

280 g (10 oz/2 cups) blanched roasted
   hazelnuts
1 tablespoon coconut cream
¼ teaspoon sea salt
30 g (1 oz) cacao powder*
2 tablespoons rice malt syrup*
1 tablespoon stevia*

ONION AND BEETROOT RELISH

Serving this on vegie burgers or just placing it on the table at a barbecue is now a must for me. This takes no time to make, is flavoursome, looks lovely and will make any relish critic happy!

Makes about 250 g (9 oz/1 cup)
Prep time: 5 minutes
Cooking time: 15 minutes

1 red onion, thinly sliced
1 tablespoon plant-based oil*
1 beetroot (beet), grated
1 green apple, peeled and
    grated
1 teaspoon balsamic vinegar
1 tablespoon coconut sugar*
1 tablespoon maple syrup
½ teaspoon salt

Sauté the onion in a frying pan over medium heat with the plant-based oil. Cook until the onion starts to become translucent then add the beetroot and apple. Cook for 5–10 minutes then add the vinegar, coconut sugar, maple syrup and salt.

Once everything is combined and coming together, remove from the heat and place the mixture in a sterilised jar.

Keep in the refrigerator for up to 2 weeks and enjoy.

ROASTED TOMATO RELISH

Makes about 250 g (9 oz/1 cup)
Prep time: 5 minutes
Cooking time: 30 minutes

Roasted tomato relish is the perfect accompaniment to many dishes. Many store-bought relishes contain numerous preservatives, additives and are packed with white sugar. This relish is easy to make, is extremely tasty and will make you forget about regular ol' tomato sauce!

300 g (10½ oz/2 cups) cherry tomatoes
2 garlic cloves, crushed
2 tablespoons plant-based oil*
½ teaspoon salt
¼ teaspoon freshly ground black pepper
1 brown onion, diced
1 teaspoon stevia*

Preheat the oven to 180°C (350°F).

In a small oven dish, place the tomatoes and garlic. Sprinkle on 1 tablespoon of the plant-based oil, salt and pepper then place in the oven for 30 minutes.

While the tomatoes are slowly roasting, in a small frying pan over medium heat cook the onion in the remaining oil. Once translucent, add the stevia, turn off the heat and set aside. Once the tomatoes are roasted, place them in a bowl with the onion. Mix together (or blitz roughly with a hand-held blender, if you like) and transfer to a sterilised jar. Allow to cool, close the lid and keep in the refrigerator for up to 1 week.

SIMPLE HOT SAUCE

Makes about 500 ml (17 fl oz/2 cups)
Prep time: 5 minutes
Cooking time: 35 minutes

I am definitely the kind of girl who always has a little bottle of hot sauce in her bag – I am addicted. This is a very simple hot sauce recipe that will last for months. It contains the perfect amount of spice and is super-easy to make. It's also great to bottle up and give as a gift – who wouldn't love a bottle of homemade hot sauce?

*4 garlic cloves, peeled but left whole
20 chillies – chipotle*, jalapeño, bird's eye or other chilli of your choice
1 teaspoon aleppo pepper*
1 teaspoon salt
1 tablespoon plant-based oil*
1 brown onion, chopped
250 ml (8½ fl oz/1 cup) white vinegar*

Combine the garlic cloves, whole chillies, aleppo pepper, salt, oil and onion in a saucepan and cook for 5 minutes over medium heat. Add 500 ml (17 fl oz/2 cups) water then reduce the heat and let simmer for 20–25 minutes until most of the liquid has evaporated. Remove the saucepan from the heat and allow to cool.

Transfer the mixture to a food processor or blender. Blitz, gradually adding the vinegar. Taste and season with extra salt and pepper as desired.

Strain and place in a sterilised jar or bottle.

For best results, let the sauce age for roughly 1–2 weeks for maximum flavour. It will last for up to 6 months in the refrigerator.

HOT SAUCE PICKLED CARROTS

Makes about 450 g (1 lb/2 cups)
Prep time: 10 minutes
Cooking time: 10 minutes

I first had Tabasco-pickled carrots when I was in San Francisco. After only eating half of one carrot (I had to share the rest with my boyfriend) I was hooked. These bad boys pack a punch and are next-level delicious! I like to serve them alongside salads, in sandwiches or as a little nibble on their own.

500 ml (17 fl oz/2 cups) apple cider vinegar
100 g (3½ oz/½ cup) coconut sugar*
1 teaspoon chilli flakes
1 teaspoon salt
2 tablespoons Simple hot sauce (page 232) or Tabasco
1 bunch baby carrots, washed with tops removed

Put the vinegar, sugar, chilli, salt and simple hot sauce in a saucepan over medium heat. Bring to the boil, then reduce the heat to very low and let simmer for 3 minutes. Add the baby carrots and cook for a further 5 minutes.

Pour the mixture into a sterilised jar and allow to cool completely.

Leave the jar on the counter with the lid off overnight, then place the lid on in the morning and transfer to the refrigerator.

These guys are best eaten a few days later, but can be eaten anytime! They keep for up to 6 months.

DILL PICKLES

Makes about 450 g
  (1 lb/2 cups)
Prep time: 10 minutes
Cooking time: 5 minutes

Pickles and I are good friends. In the distant past, I was never the gal who would fling the pickles out of a burger and I certainly would never refuse a good pickle now. Making your own pickles is super-easy and it's a great condiment to add many dishes or platters.

500 ml (17 fl oz/2 cups) apple cider vinegar
100 g (3½ oz/½ cup) coconut sugar*
1 teaspoon salt
½ teaspoon chilli flakes
350 g (12½ oz/2 cups) baby cucumbers (about 8–10)
15 g (½ oz/¼ cup) dill
3 garlic cloves, peeled

Combine the vinegar, coconut sugar, salt and chilli in a small saucepan over medium heat and bring to the boil. Once boiling, reduce the heat to low and continue to simmer for 5 minutes.

Place the baby cucumbers in a large sterilised jar with the dill and garlic cloves. Pour the vinegar mixture over the cucumbers and leave to cool with the lid off overnight.

Place in the refrigerator and eat as you like! Keep for up to 6 months.

WHIPPED COCONUT CREAM

Prep time: 5 minutes
Makes about 480 g
  (1 lb 1 oz/ 2 cups)

When I first discovered that coconut cream whips, I felt as if the clouds had disappeared and the sun was shining down on my kitchen. What a beautiful discovery and what an amazing healthy alternative to regular dairy cream! Just make sure you keep your tins of coconut cream in the refrigerator before making this, as the coconut cream needs to be cold to whip.

400 ml (13½ fl oz) coconut cream, refrigerated overnight
1–2 tablespoons stevia*
seeds from 1 vanilla bean

Pour the coconut cream into an electric mixer and whip on a high speed with the stevia and vanilla seeds. Allow to whip until completely thickened, just as dairy whipped cream would be.

Use immediately or store in the refrigerator for up to 3–5 days.

COCONUT 'DULCE DE LECHE'

Makes about 325 g (11½ oz/ 1 cup)
Prep time: 5 minutes
Cooking time: 30–40 minutes

This is one of the best things to come out of my kitchen. I am obsessed with this sweet spread. Since discovering this divine and intense caramel I have wanted to use it in everything! Like all great caramels, it's wonderful in so many desserts. Give it a go and begin your addiction to dulce de leche, the healthy version!

400 ml (13½ fl oz) tin coconut cream
100 g (3½ oz/1 cup) coconut sugar*
½ teaspoon salt

Pour the coconut cream into a small saucepan with the sugar and salt. Simmer over low heat, string occasionally, for 30–40 minutes until thickened and a caramel colour.

Place in a sterilised jar and keep in the refrigerator for up to 2 weeks.

INGREDIENT GUIDE

agar agar
A substance made from algae that can be used in place of gelatine to make jellies, panna cotta etc. It is plant-based and vegan-friendly. You can find agar agar in health food shops, organic supermarkets and online.

aleppo pepper
A crushed pepper made from the aleppo or halaby pepper, commonly used in Middle Eastern and Mediterannean cooking. It has a mild flavour with a medium spice and can be found in specialty Mediterranean and/or Middle Eastern shops and online. This is my favourite type of crushed red pepper or chilli.

amaranth
A gluten-free seed derived from a species of the *Amaranthus* genus. It is high in protein and looks similar to couscous. You can find it in a puffed form or its original seed form in supermarkets, health food stores and online.

bee pollen
Bee pollen is a mass pollen created by honeybees in granule form. Each granule contains over 2 million flower pollen grains. It's high in amino acids and protein, vitamins and folic acid. It can be found in health food stores, organic supermarkets and online. However the more local it is, the better the benefits are for your body!

black rice
A form of rice that is black in colour (or purple once cooked). It is high in iron, vitamin E and antioxidants. It is available in supermarkets, health food stores and online.

brown rice crisps
Brown rice crisps are made from brown rice that has been puffed and crisped. It is available in the cereal section of health food and organic stores and available online. Note – there are brown rice puffs and brown rice crisps, and a different process has been used for each, resulting in two different products.

brown rice noodles
Flat Asian noodles made from brown rice. They are a great gluten-free alternative to regular noodles and can be used in Asian cooking, salads and soups. They are a good source of protein and dietary fibre. Available in selected health food stores and online.

buckwheat groats
Not to be confused with wheat, buckwheat groats are the seeds derived from a flowering plant. Buckwheat groats can also be ground into flour form, which is great as a gluten-free substitute for wheat flour in baking. Available in most supermarkets, health food stores and online.

cacao butter
Made from cacao beans, cacao butter is the result of cold-pressing the oil from the bean. It is the base ingredient of chocolate and is also used in skin care products. It is available for purchase in health food stores, organic supermarkets and online.

cacao nibs
Cacao nibs are cacao beans that have been separated from their husks and broken into smaller chocolate chip-sized pieces. They are the rawest form of chocolate you

will find and are high in antioxidants and magnesium. You can use cacao nibs as a substitute for chocolate chips in any recipe, and enjoy the flavour of dark chocolate with all the nutritional benefits. Available in some supermarkets, health food stores, organic supermarkets and online.

cacao powder

Cacao powder is the result of pulverising the raw cacao beans and separating the powder from the cacao butter. This is the raw version of cocoa and still has all the nutrients of the cacao bean. Use it as a replacement for cocoa for a huge boost of nutrients in your food. Available in supermarkets, health food stores, organic supermarkets and online.

caramelised buckwheat

Buckwheat groats that have been coated in a low-fructose sweetener and either dehydrated or toasted to create a crunchy, caramelised product. Available in health food stores, organic supermarkets and online.

carob powder

Commonly known as the replacement for chocolate, carob is a pod that can be eaten whole or dried and ground into a powder. The powder can then be used as a replacement for cocoa/cacao. Available in health food stores, organic supermarkets and online.

chana masala

Chana masala is a spice mix that is commonly used in Indian and Pakistani cuisine. It is comprised of numerous other spices and is available to buy in supermarkets, Indian grocers and online. It can be added to curries or vegetables before roasting.

chia seeds, black chia seeds

Chia seeds are high in omega-3 fatty acids and come from the chia plant. When soaked in water they can be used as a vegan egg replacement or turned into a pudding-like dish. They can be sprinkled into smoothies, cereals and numerous other foods. Find them in supermarkets, health food stores and online.

chipotle chilli, dried and smoked

Chipotle chillies are smoked and dried jalapeños. They are quite hot, have a distinct smoky flavour and are used most commonly in Mexican cuisine. They can be found at Latin grocers and online.

coconut nectar

Coconut nectar is a liquid sweetener produced from coconut palm blossoms. It is a low GI sweetener and has a delicious taste. It is a good sugar alternative in both its sustainability factors and health benefits. Available from health food stores, organic grocers and online.

coconut sugar

Coconut sugar is the evaporated granular form of coconut nectar. It has a low GI and is derived from the coconut palm blossom. It is a good sugar and brown sugar alternative and has a rich caramel-like taste. Available from most supermarkets, grocers and online.

date paste

Date paste is made from medjool dates that have been puréed on their own or with a bit of water to create a paste. This is a perfect sugar replacement in baking and is also great added to smoothies and ice creams. You can buy this at supermarkets, health food stores or create your own at home.

dragon fruit

Dragon fruit is an Asian fruit that is high in fibre and low in calories. It is either yellow- or red- (hot pink-) skinned with a white or red-speckled flesh. It is high in vitamin C and antioxidants. It can be found in warmer seasons at markets, Asian grocers and some supermarkets.

edamame

Edamame are the immature soy bean pods used in many Asian cuisines. They can be bought in pod form or just as the beans. They can be eaten as a snack or added to salads, stir-fries and other dishes. Find them in some greengrocers and Asian supermarkets.

enoki mushrooms

A small, long white mushroom primarily used in Asian cooking. It has a mild and somewhat crunchy texture. Use enoki mushrooms in salads, soups, stir-fries and many other dishes. They can be found in most supermarkets and Asian grocers.

flaked brown rice

Brown rice flakes are made from short-grain brown rice. The rice is fire-roasted then rolled into flakes. The flakes can be used as an alternative to oats for porridges and other dishes and are a great source of magnesium, vitamin B3 and fibre. Available from health food stores, organic grocers and online.

flaxmeal/flax eggs

Flaxmeal is created by grinding flaxseeds (also commonly known as linseeds) into a powder-like form. This meal is high in omega-3 fatty acids and rich in antioxidants and fibre. It can be used to create an egg replacement in vegan cooking by soaking 1 tablespoon flaxmeal with 60 ml (¼ cup) water. Available from supermarkets, health food stores and organic grocers.

flaxseed oil

Flaxseed oil is a light coloured oil derived from flaxseeds (linseeds). It is a good source of omega-3 and omega-6 fatty acids and can be used in raw dishes or added to smoothies. Flaxseed oil should not be heated. It is available from health food stores, organic grocers and online.

flaxseeds

Also known as linseeds, flaxseeds are a great source of fibre, omega-3 fatty acids and antioxidants. They can be ground into a meal form to use in cooking, sprinkled into smoothies or other dishes or cold-pressed into an oil form. Available from supermarkets, health food stores and organic grocers.

garlic and ginger paste

Garlic and ginger paste is simply blended garlic and ginger. Available at most supermarkets, Indian grocers and Asian grocers.

gluten-free puff pastry

Puff pastry that is made with non-glutinous flours. It is sold in sheet form. Available from supermarkets, health food stores and organic grocers.

grain-sweetened chocolate

Grain-sweetened chocolate is chocolate that is sweetened with rice malt instead of sugar. It is available in some health food stores and online.

guar gum

This is the ground-up powder of the guar bean. It can be used in cooking as a thickener and is eight times stronger than cornflour (cornstarch). It's often used to help in making doughs. Available from health food stores and organic grocers.

hemp seeds

The seeds derived from the hemp plant. They are high in omega-3 and omega-6 fatty acids, are very high in protein and a number of vitamins and minerals. They are easy to digest and have a soft nutty texture and taste. They can be used to make milk, eaten as a snack or sprinkled onto different foods. Available at health food stores, organic grocers and online.

hibiscus vinegar

A healthy vinegar made using the beautiful hibiscus flower. It is great to use on salads or to add flavour to many dishes. Available in specialty grocers and online.

kuzu

Kuzu is the root of a plant found in Japan and is grown in mountainous regions. It is used in cooking as a thickening agent for both sweet and savoury dishes. It comes in a powdery rock form, which can be crushed into a powder. It can help alkalise the body and is great as a thickener in vegan and vegetarian cooking. It can be found in health food stores and online.

liquid probiotics

These are found in health food stores and online and are most commonly used to help gut bacteria and restore healthy digestion. They can be consumed on their own or added to milk or coconut milk to create a fermented, probiotic-rich yoghurt.

lucuma

Lucuma powder has a caramel-like taste and is created from the Peruvian fruit of the same name. It is rich in fibre, carbohydrates, vitamins and minerals. It is great used in cooking, for example added to smoothies and desserts. It can also be used as a low GI sweetener alternative. It's rich in antioxidants, has anti-inflammatory properties and is said to help in the healing of wounds and in anti-ageing. It can be found at health food stores, specialty grocers and online.

maca

Maca powder is made from the maca root, and is most commonly known for its energising and revitalising nature. It is packed with vitamins and minerals and can help in supporting the immune system, boosting the metabolism, increasing energy, helping balance hormones and normalising menstrual cycles. It can be found in some supermarkets, health food stores and online.

masa harina

A finely ground corn flour used in Spanish and Mexican cooking. Masa harina can be found in health food stores, Latin grocers and online.

matcha

Matcha powder is a fine green tea powder that has been made using the whole green tea leaf. It is known for its metabolism-enhancing and stress-reducing effects and its high antioxidant count. It is often used in Asian cultures to make a nutrient-filled drink, but can be added to cooking to make delicious green tea-flavoured foods. It is available from health food stores, Asian grocers and online.

medjool dates

Medjool dates are a variety of fruit grown on date palm trees. They are commonly found dried or semi-dried and are one of the larger date varieties. They are rich in flavour and are great used as a sweetener in cooking or eaten as a snack on their own. They have an almost caramel-like flavour and are rich in minerals and fibre. They are found in supermarkets and health food stores.

mesquite powder

Mesquite powder is extracted from the seeds of the mesquite plant found most commonly in South America. It is great used as a sweetener and has a subtle molasses-like flavour. It is rich in minerals and amino acids and is high in protein and soluble fibre. It is very low GI and is great used in cooking, added to smoothies or desserts.

It can be found in health food stores, specialty grocers and online.

miso paste
A thick spread made from fermented soy beans. It is used as a staple in Japanese cooking and is great in soups, stir-fries, curries and more. It is available from supermarkets, health food stores and specialty grocers.

nori
An edible seaweed that is most commonly sold in sheets and used for sushi. It is high in vitamins A and C and is often used in Japanese cooking. It is available at supermarkets, health food stores and specialty grocers.

pink lake salt
An all-natural Australian salt that has been harvested from the pink lake in western Victoria. It is packed with nutrients and minerals, including calcium, iron, magnesium and zinc. It is available from some supermarkets, health food stores, specialty grocers and online.

plant-based milk
Any milk derived from a plant. Soy, hemp, almond, cashew, coconut and rice are all examples of plant-derived milks.

plant-based oil
Oils, such as macadamia, olive, coconut, walnut and hemp, which are derived from plants, as opposed to animal sources. It is important to choose a healthy non-GMO plant-based oil when cooking as it is the crucial base of many recipes. Look for a high smoke point oil when cooking with heat, such as macadamia or avocado. If using mild heat, use olive oil. When cooking raw or low-heat foods, look for oils like hemp or flaxseed. Avoid vegetable, canola and sunflower oils where possible, as they can be highly GMO.

plant-based protein powder
Protein powder derived from plant protein sources.

pomegranate vinegar
A tangy and delicious vinegar that is high in tannins and antioxidants. It is often used in Mediterranean cooking and is great in salad dressings. It is available from some supermarkets, health food stores and specialty grocers.

potato starch
The starch extracted from potatoes, which is often found in powder form and used in cooking as a thickener and in gluten-free baking. It is available from health food stores, specialty grocers and online.

psyllium husks
Pysllium husks are a high source of dietary fibre derived from the husks of the seeds of the plant *Plantago ovata*. It is commonly used to help with bowel and constipation issues, and is a flavourless powder that can be added to almost any food or drink. It is available at supermarkets, health food stores and online.

quinoa (for those not yet in the know!)
A seed that comes from a plant closely related to beetroot (beet) and spinach. It is high in protein, magnesium, iron, fibre, is gluten-free and is great used in cooking as an alternative to glutinous carbs. Quinoa can be used as a replacement for oats in porridge, can be cooked in water to use as a rice replacement or added to salads. It is a very versatile and tasty nutritional seed. Available from supermarkets, health food stores and online.

rice malt syrup

A syrup made from brown rice. It is a healthy alternative to sugar and contains zero fructose. It has a honey-like consistency and is great used in cooking or even as a spread. It is gluten-free and contains complex carbohydrates. It is available from most supermarkets, health food stores and organic grocers.

rose water syrup

A syrup made made using water and rose petals, which can be found in most supermarkets and specialty markets. It is great added to desserts and drinks.

savoury yeast

Deactivated yeast with a strong cheesy taste. It is very rich in vitamin B and is sold in the form of flakes or powder. It is a great alternative to cheese for vegetarians and vegans and can be sprinkled onto dishes or added to nut cheeses for a stronger flavour. It is sold in health food stores, organic grocers and online.

stevia

Stevia is one of my favourite sweeteners and can be bought from your local nursery in its plant form, or found on supermarket or health food store shelves in a granulated or liquid form. It is a plant-based sweetener derived from the stevia plant. It has zero kilojoules (calories) and zero fructose. It is a great sugar substitute.

tapioca flour

Tapioca is a gluten-free, grain-free flour derived from the cassava root. It is a starchy flour often used in gluten-free baking. It can improve the texture in cooking and is used as a thickener in many dishes, used in place of cornflour (cornstarch). Available from health food stores, organic grocers and online.

wakame

Wakame is a variety of sea vegetable/seaweed. It comes most often in freeze-dried form and is used across many Japanese and Asian dishes. It is high in magnesium and calcium and is great added to soups, salads and Asian meals. It is available from health food stores, Asian grocers and online.

xylitol

A sweetener with very low GI and very few kilojoules (calories). It is a great sugar alternative to use in cooking and does not have an aftertaste. It can be found in health food stores, organic grocers and online.

INDEX

My heart is filled with so much love for everyone who held my hand through the making of this book. I feel very lucky and extremely grateful that I was supported to the extent I was on every step of this journey.

While there are many people I need to give my heart to, the first person I must thank is my beautiful photographer Elisa Watson. This girl spent countless hours, days, weeks and even months photographing my food and lending her time. She has been with me since day one of Kenkō and never once stopped believing in me or inspiring me. I definitely would not be where I am today if it were not for this human!

The second person I need to express my gratitude for, of course, is my amazing mother, Roni. I really don't know what I would have done if I didn't have her with me through this journey. She has been my kitchen hand, my DIY props maker, my recipe tester, my chauffeur, my personal shopper, my shrink as well as being my mum. This woman never stopped inspiring me, doing things to help me and was always there to hug me when I was about to throw my food in the bin and give up.

I would also like to thank my sister, Sally, for giving up countless weekends to help me style the photos. Without her touch I wouldn't have many of the great photos in this book. She is a total legend and definitely the master of pea placement!

Thank you to my faithful partner, Bulut, for all his supermarket and farmers' market runs, as well as for cleaning, washing dishes and helping with whatever I needed. He always stayed up late with me when I had deadlines and was always there to make me smile and laugh when I needed it.

Thank you to Belle Gibson for being more than my best friend, but also being a beautiful mentor and inspiration. She constantly gives me the inspiration and confidence to want to create and do good in the world. This woman has achieved things I never even thought possible and continues to fight for our right to accessible health and wellness on a daily basis. She is incredible.

Thank you to my dad, Ross, and my brother, Tim, for being the mouths to test my food. Thank you to Greta and Diem for being my number one vegan inspirations (and for all your recipe contributions and your inspiring pure heart Diem). To my pooches Waz and Reggie for always being my ever faithful kitchen hands and accidental food testers.

I would like to thank Joseph Monroe, Dustin Bailey, Catie Gett, Lisa Marie Corso, Lucy Clairmont, Clive Rothwell, Daniel Hillier, Rosie and Shari Hart, Adam Thompson and all my instagram followers, subscribers and everyone else who always supported me and believed in me and Kenkō.

Finally I would like to thank the team at Hardie Grant for believing in me from so early on in the piece and for giving me this opportunity. Thank you to Paul McNally for making everything possible, Hannah Koelmeyer for keeping me on track and to Mark Campbell for your design work. Thank you to the whole team for all your patience and guidance throughout this process, making it so easy and seamless. This is an incredible team and it's been a pleasure to make this book with them. And last but not least, to the amazing Ariana Klepac, who helped turn all my nonsensical writings into something decipherable and for being a great and understanding human!

I just love and thank everyone!!

Published in 2015 by Hardie Grant Books

Hardie Grant Books (Australia)
Ground Floor, Building 1
658 Church Street
Richmond, Victoria 3121
www.hardiegrant.com.au

Hardie Grant Books (UK)
5th & 6th Floor
52–54 Southwark Street
London SE1 1RU
www.hardiegrant.co.uk

All rights reserved. No part of this publication may be reproduced, stored in a retrieval
system or transmitted in any form by any means, electronic, mechanical, photocopying,
recording or otherwise, without the prior written permission of the publishers and
copyright holders.

The moral rights of the author have been asserted.

Copyright text © Kate Bradley 2015
Copyright photography © Elisa Watson 2015
Copyright design © Hardie Grant Books 2015

A Cataloguing-in-Publication entry is available from the catalogue of the National Library
of Australia at www.nla.gov.au
Kenkō Kitchen
9781742708461

Publishing Director: Paul McNally
Project Editor: Hannah Koelmeyer
Editor: Ariana Klepac
Designer: Mark Campbell
Photographer: Elisa Watson
Food preparation and styling: Kate Bradley
Production Manager: Todd Rechner

Colour reproduction by Splitting Image Colour Studio
Printed and bound in China by 1010 Printing International Limited

Find this book on **Cooked.**
cooked.com.au
cooked.co.uk